MICHELANGELO

This is a Parragon Publishing Book
This edition published in 2004

Parragon Publishing
Queen Street House
4 Queen Street
Bath BA1 1HE, UK

Copyright © Parragon 2000

ISBN:1-40542-984-4

The right of Kirsten Bradbury to be identified as the author of this work
has been asserted in accordance with Section 77 of the Copyright,
Designs and Patents Act of 1988.

The right of Lucinda Hawksley to be identified as the author of the
introduction to this book has been asserted in accordance with Section
77 of the Copyright, Designs and Patents Act of 1988.

Printed and bound in China.

MICHELANGELO

KIRSTEN BRADBURY

Introduction by Lucinda Hawksley

p

CONTENTS

Introduction 6
Copy of the Sagra del Carmine 16
Two Figures after Giotto 18
Madonna of the Steps 20
Battle of Hercules with the Centaurs 22
Bacchus 24
Satyr (Detail from Bacchus) 26
Pietà, St Peter's 28
The Virgin's Head (Detail from Pietà) 30
David 32
Face (Detail from David) 34
Doni Tondo (The Holy Family) 36
St John the Baptist (Detail from The Holy Family) 38
Study for the Doni Madonna 40
St Peter 42
The Madonna of Bruges 44
The Pitti Tondo 46
The Taddei Tondo 48
Study for The Battle of Cascina 50
Study for a Figure from the Battle of Cascina 52
St Matthew 54
Male Nude (Full Facing) 56
Two Nude Men Raising a Third Man 58
The Virgin, St Anne and Male Nude 60
Different Studies of Figures 62
Sistine Chapel 64
Sistine Chapel Ceiling 66
The Separation of Light from Darkness 68
The Creation of the Planets, the Sun and the Moon 70
The Separation of the Earth from the Waters 72
The Creation of Adam 74
The Creation of Adam 76
The Hand of God (Detail from The Creation of Adam) . . . 78
The Creation of Eve 80
The Creation of Eve and the Prophet Ezekiel 82
The Fall of Man and the Expulsion from Paradise 84
The Snake and the Expulsion (Detail from The Fall of Man) . . 86
The Sacrifice of Noah 88
The Flood 90
The Drunkenness of Noah 92
Ignudi Between the Drunkenness of Noah and the Flood 94
Ignudo between the Drunkenness of Noah and the Flood 96
Ignudo near the Sacrifice of Noah 98
Ignudo by the Drunkenness of Noah 100
Ignudo by the Libyan Sibyl 102
The Ancestors of Christ 104
Ancestor of Christ 106
Esther and Haman 108
Judith Carrying the Head of Holofernes 110
The Persian Sibyl 112
The Cumaean Sibyl 114
The Erithraean Sibyl 116
The Delphic Sibyl 118
The Libyan Sibyl 120
The Prophet Zachariah 122
The Prophet Ezekiel 124
The Prophet Joel 126
The Prophet Jeremiah 128
The Prophet Isaiah 130
The Prophet Daniel 132
The Ancestors of Christ (Detail showing David and Goliath) . 134
The Risen Christ 136
Tomb of Pope Julius II 138
Design for the Tomb of Pope Julius II 140

CONTENTS

Moses (Detail from the Tomb of Pope Julius II) 142
Rachel and Leah (Detail from the Tomb of Pope Julius II) 144
Dying Slave 146
Rebellious Slave 148
Awakening Slave 150
Bearded Slave 152
Young Slave 154
Victory 156
Head (Detail from Victory) 158
Three Virile Nudes 160
Interior of the Medici Chapel 162
Study for the Medici Chapel 164
Tomb of Lorenzo de' Medici 166
Madonna and Child 168
Giuliano de' Medici 170
Night 172
Day 174
Lorenzo of Urbino 176
Dawn 178
Dusk 180
Laurentian Library, Reading Room 182
Laurentian Library, Staircase 184
Apollo 186
Detail from Apollo 188
Hercules and Cacus 190
Ideal Head 192
Study of a Man Shouting 194
The Fall of Phaeton 196
The Dead Christ 198
Sketch of a Male Head and Two Legs 200
The Last Judgment 202
Detail of Christ from The Last Judgment 204
Detail of the Blessed from The Last Judgment 206
Detail of Angels from The Last Judgment 208
Study for The Last Judgment 210
Detail of The Sinners from The Last Judgment 212
Detail of St Bartholomew from The Last Judgment 214
Detail of Charon from The Last Judgment 216
Piazza del Campidoglio 218
Bust of Brutus 220
Sacrifice of Isaac 222
The Crucifixion of Christ 224
Head of Christ 226
Study of Madonna and Child 228
St Mary Magdalene Contemplating the Crown of Thorns 230
The Conversion of St Paul 232
The Crucifixion of St Peter 234
Inner Courtyard, Palazzo Farnese 236
Interior of the Dome of St Peter's Basilica 238
Duomo Pietà 240
Study for the Holy Family (Epifania) 242
Study for Christ on the Cross (with the Virgin and St John) 244
Palestrina Pietà 246
Head of Cleopatra 248
The Rondanini Pietà 250
St Peter's Basilica 252
St Peter's Basilica 254
Acknowledgements 256

INTRODUCTION

MICHELANGELO Buonarroti was born on March 6, 1475. He lived for almost a full century and died on February 18, 1564; he was still working six days before his death. During his life, the western world underwent what was perhaps the most remarkable period of change since the decline of the Roman Empire. The Renaissance saw changes in all aspects of life and culture, with dramatic reforms sweeping through the worlds of religion, politics, and scientific belief. Michelangelo was one of the most fervent advocates of this exciting new philosophy, working with a remarkable energy that was mirrored by contemporary society.

He was born at Caprese, in Tuscany, the second of five sons of Lodovico di Leonardo (a civil servant) and Francesca Buonarroti. The family had two homes: one in the Tuscan countryside, and a much smaller one in the city of Florence. In 1481, when Michelangelo was six years old, his mother died. 1481 was to be a portentous year in more ways than one, as it was also the year in which he had his first drawing lesson from a local artist named Francesco Granacci.

In 1488, at the age of 13, Michelangelo moved to Florence and began working as an assistant to Domenico Ghirlandaio (1449–94), who had recently started work on Florence's Santa Maria Novella church. In 1489, after completing just one year of his

apprenticeship, Michelangelo came to the attention of Lorenzo de' Medici, who summoned the boy to his court. There, he was free to wander the gardens at will, drinking in all the fine examples of Classical statuary owned by the Medicis. It was there that he began to learn the secrets of sculpting, teaching himself by making drawings of the statues and attempting to recreate them in clay. He was aided in his studies by the elderly curator of the gardens, Bertoldo di Giovanni (c. 1420–91), who had formerly studied under the master sculptor Donatello (c. 1386–1466).

Through his association with the court of Lorenzo, Michelangelo was in contact with the most brilliant thinkers, artists, and writers of his day. This experience was to enrich his life and consciousness. He was not only an artist, architect, and sculptor; he also wrote proficiently, producing countless poems and letters in his lifetime. Other influences on his young mind included two members of the church: one was his local priest, who, in return for the gift of a crucifix the young sculptor had carved, allowed him access to the bodies kept at the church so that he could study anatomy; the other

formative influence was an articulate and opinionated monk named Fra Girolamo Savonarola (1452–98). He was a zealous reformer and an outspoken preacher; he was later to become the moral dictator of Florence for several months after the flight of the Medicis in 1494. He ruled by instilling religious fear into the Florentine people, foretelling great disaster if God was offended. His blistering sermons scalded many facets of Renaissance society and implicated many of the most powerful people of the day. This led to his eventual excommunication and execution in 1498; he was burnt at the stake in the Piazza della Signoria, where Michelangelo's *David* was later to stand.

Michelangelo first heard Savonarola preach in 1492, the year in which his first patron, Lorenzo de' Medici, died and Michelangelo returned to his father's home. The monk's sermons and his subsequent violent death had a lifelong effect on the artist and many of his works; the loss of Lorenzo also deeply affected his artistic consciousness.

By the age of 16, Michelangelo had begun to produce his own works. These included *Madonna of the Steps* (1491–92) and the *Battle of Hercules with the Centaurs* (1491–92). These two pieces, although of a similar date, are vastly different from one another: the *Battle* abounds with aggression and vitality, it teems with writhing, undulating shapes filling every section of the marble with boundless energy; in contrast, the *Madonna* is serenely tranquil, containing little movement within an

unfinished relief created to invoke an atmosphere of gentleness.

In 1494, Florence suffered severe political upheaval. Until that time, it had been a separate city state led by the powerful Medici family, but in 1494 the city was invaded by the French king, Charles VIII. The political climate for intimates of the Medici circle became troubled, and when news of the forthcoming French invasion reached Florence, Michelangelo, like many other prominent Florentines, fled the city before the troops arrived. First, he traveled to Venice and then to Bologna, before he felt able to return home in 1495. While in Bologna, he was commissioned to complete a sculpture that had remained unfinished for 200 years, the tomb of St Dominic, Bologna's patron saint. The piece was begun by the sculptor Nicola Pisano (c. 1284–1314), but three figures needed adding. These were freestanding statues—the first of Michelangelo's career: St Proculus, St Petronius, and an angel.

Michelangelo's work for the Medici family continued after the invasion of Florence. At the age of 21, he made his first trip to Rome—a city that was both to play a prominent part in his life and create many frustrations for him. This time he spent five years in the city, creating some of his best-known works. In 1496–97 he completed his first important commission, Bacchus. As was his wont, the sculptor depicted the god of wine in a way never seen before. In place of the usual vision of *Bacchus*, an omnipotent force, genial but capable of brutality if crossed, Michelangelo sculpted a decadent, stupefied, almost effeminate drunk. Typically of his work, Bacchus's anatomy is executed superbly, the fluidity of the back muscles suggesting he has only just slipped into his drunken posture. It is a world away from previous depictions of the god and from the attractive, youthful *Bacchus* of Jacopo Sansovino (1486–1570), created just 15 years later, which reverts to the traditional Classical method that Michelangelo had considered outdated.

In 1497–98, Michelangelo created the *Pietà*, a masterpiece of sculpture that could not be farther removed in content from the witty *Bacchus*. The *Pietà* is heralded as one of his greatest achievements. The sorrowing face of Mary, contemplating the lifeless body of her eldest child, still wrings the heart today. He took the subject out of a religious context and placed it in a humanist light, emphaszsing the grief of Mary and the mortality of her dead son.

On August 4, 1501, the turbulence of previous years seemed to come to an end and the city of Florence was declared a republic. On August 16, the new republic commissioned Michelangelo to make the statue of *David*. He was asked to sculpt it from a single block of marble; one that had been worked on 40 years previously by Agostino di Duccio, but had been left unfinished.

David is perhaps the world's most famous statue and a cult has grown up around it. When one views this sixteenth-century masterpiece, it is apparent what all the fuss is about. Michelangelo's command of anatomy is superb; every muscle is painstakingly defined, every movement understood by the artist. Traditionally, works on this subject show a diminutive David standing by the severed head of the defeated Goliath; Michelangelo chose to change the perspective of this time-honored myth. His *David*, his face determined and thoughtful, stands strongly and pensively waiting to attack the giant. His hand holds the shot, his sling hangs over his back. Michelangelo captures the brief moment of reflection on the hero's face, showing tremendous concentration as he decides how to save his people. The subject matter was apt for the Florentines, themselves on the brink of a new era, having recently been freed from a political dinosaur.

On September 8, 1504, the completed sculpture was taken to the Piazza della Signoria in the center of Florence, where it was placed in front of the Palazzo Vecchio. Such was the impact of Michelangelo's creation that it changed Florentine law—becoming the first naked statue to be allowed on public display since Classical times. Today, the original is housed in the Galleria della Accademia, but a copy also remains in the Piazza della Signoria in the heart of Florence.

In 1505, Michelangelo was summoned to Rome on the orders of Pope Julius II, who ruled between 1503 and 1513. He was a member of one of the most important families in Italy—the della Rovere family, political rivals of the Medicis. Hungry for earthly immortality, Julius commissioned Michelangelo to make his tomb; a monument of vast and expensive proportions, which was intended to be finished within five years.

The next few years were to be the most frustrating and miserable of Michelangelo's life, in which he found himself at the mercy of an inconsistent, temperamental authoritarian. The power of the pope forbade Michelangelo to leave Rome, even though he was unable to begin working on the tomb: Julius stalled the project through his indecision as to where the great edifice was to be placed. In preparation for his own death, the pope began an extensive recreation of St Peter's cathedral, intending to rest in supreme state for eternity—meanwhile Michelangelo was left in a state of limbo.

Relations with the pope eased when, on May 10, 1508, Julius gave Michelangelo a new commission, which drastically changed the way in which he saw himself and his art. Until now he had been, by definition, a sculptor, yet the pope commissioned him to fresco the ceiling of the Sistine Chapel. Michelangelo had to learn the art of painting, just as he had had to do with sculpture as a teenager. He found this arduous and disheartening; a letter sent to his father in 1509 records his extreme frustration:

"… my work does not seem to go ahead [as I would like it to] … This is due to the difficulty of the work and

also because it is not my profession. In consequence, I lose my time fruitlessly. May God help me."

The frustrated artist looked to his former master, Ghirlandaio, for assistance with the technique of fresco painting, in 1481–82. Ghirlandaio had begun the task of painting the Sistine Chapel ceiling in 1481 before his death in 1494. Between 1508 and 1512, Michelangelo painted over 300 figures onto the ceiling. As with *David* and *Bacchus*, the scenes were not always depicted in the expected, conventional, and traditional manner of the time. This is most notable in his *Garden of Eden* fresco, where both Adam and Eve are seen as equally culpable for their downfall after eating from the

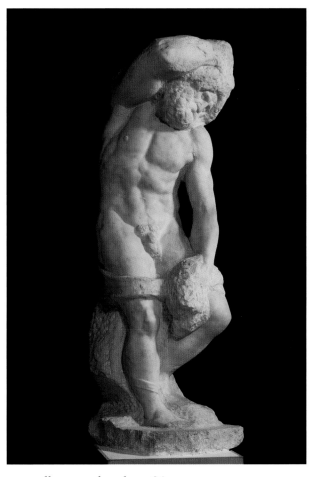

Tree of Knowledge. The ceiling was eventually completed on 21 October 1512; a task that was arduous in the extreme.

In 1513, Pope Julius III died—his magnificent tomb still unfinished—leaving Michelangelo to continue discussions about the tomb with his more agreeable heirs. However, the tomb was to suffer further setbacks for much of the sculptor's life. After the death of Pope Julius II, Giovanni de' Medici was ordained as Pope Leo X. He remained in power for ten years. Michelangelo's links with the Medici family had remained strong and Pope Leo determined to keep the association going—not least to prevent the harried artist from having any free time in which to work on the tomb of a della Rovere.

The reign of Leo X was liberating to Michelangelo. Within a couple of years of Leo's election, he was back in his beloved Florence, free to live where he chose and still to undertake prestigious projects for the new pope. Meanwhile, Julius II's tomb was planned and replanned several times—each new drawing diminishing the tomb in size from previous plans and becoming less and less ornate.

Michelangelo made his home in Florence from 1515 until 1534. During this time, the city once again suffered massive upheavals. Since the time of Charles VIII's invasion and the city's subsequent republican status, the Medici family had returned. Although originally supported by the Medicis, Michelangelo was a fervent supporter of the republic. In 1527, the Medicis were driven from Florence once more, and the city declared a republic for a second time. Michelangelo was among several prominent Florentines who foresaw great political times ahead. He was appointed Governor of the Fortifications, a position that he took great pride in, although the rapid return to power of the Medicis thwarted his political ambitions. In 1530, the Medicis, aided by King Charles V of Spain, were restored to long-term power in Florence.

The year 1530 also saw a new commission for Michelangelo, given by Baccio Valori, the hugely unpopular governor of the Florentine republic. The result of this commission was the work that has become known as *David (Apollo)*, owing to uncertainty about which figure it represents. There are arguments for both and, with no concrete evidence, the art world will never be able to decide for certain. If it was intended as David—some critics suggest this because the crude round shape on which the figure's foot rests may have been intended as an unfinished head of Goliath—it is significantly inferior to his earlier masterpiece. This has often been cited as indicative of Michelangelo's dislike of his patron Valori; he often used his art as a medium to express his opinions of people. For instance, he incorporated recognizable portraits in the ceiling of the Sistine Chapel, using the character of the painted figure to suggest his like or dislike of the person intimated. He also incorporated his own face into his work at times—his self-portrait can be discerned in several of his works.

In 1532, Michelangelo paid one of his frequent visits to Rome. Here, at the age of 57, he fell in love with a young nobleman called Tommaso de' Cavalieri. Two years later, he decided to leave Florence and settle in Rome. Cavalieri was extremely handsome, and as one who strove to create beauty in his art, Michelangelo saw his lover as God's most perfect artwork, describing him as the "paragon of all the world." Much of their correspondence survives, as does the poetry that the sculptor wrote to his lover. His creative energy now had a new outlet, which complemented his prolific output. The two men remained close until Michelangelo's death.

Another important friend of the artist was a widow named Vittoria Colonna, Marchioness of Pescara. She was a deeply religious woman and a Catholic reformer, whose forward-thinking views held abundant interest for Michelangelo. He wrote her some of his most evocative poetry and, until her death in 1547, the two were extremely close—some sources suggest they were lovers, while others see it as an impassioned friendship. Michelangelo, as a poet, was strongly influenced by the work of yet another famous Florentine, the revered Dante Alighieri (1265–1321). During his early exile from Florence, in the time of King Charles VIII's invasion,

and subsequently, during his enforced time in Rome under Pope Julius II, Michelangelo must have felt kinship with Dante, who had also been exiled. In his poetry to and about Vittoria, Michelangelo often compared her to Beatrice Portinari, the eulogized object of Dante's love. He also produced some of his finest religious drawings for Vittoria, in particular a masterful *Pietà*, drawn in 1546, just one year before she died. The distraught but powerful mother of Christ sits with her arms outstretched, embodying the cross from which her son has just been removed. The dead Christ is slumped between her knees—supported on either side by a robust, sorrowful *putto*—his head bowed with the sins of the world, his limbs loose in death. Both mother and son are powerfully drawn, with Christ's figure utilizing Michelangelo's fine command of anatomy. From the start of his friendship with Vittoria Colonna, Michelangelo's work became more religious in content, and his poetry and art also became more concerned with death.

Michelangelo's time in Rome was filled with commissions—alongside which he was still attempting to finish the long- term project of the tomb of Pope Julius II. This was eventually unveiled in 1547; it

had taken 42 years to reach completion. While in Rome, he was appointed Chief Architect of St Peter's in the Vatican and was commissioned to paint the frescoes in the Vatican's Pauline Chapel (Pope Paul III's private chapel).

The works of Michelangelo are an intimate insight into the superb mind of a remarkable man; a man who, even in his own lifetime, was revered as a genius. His contemporary and biographer, Giorgio Vasari (1511–74), wrote of him as "the divine Michelangelo," describing him as a 'master' who "surpasses and excels" not only the artists of his own time, but also all artists who came before, including the great sculptors of antiquity.

Michelangelo was a deeply spiritual man, whose genius came in part from his observations of the many different forces to which he was exposed throughout his extraordinary life. It came from the teenage years spent at the court of Lorenzo de' Medici—who was a prominent humanist and forward-thinking leader of Renaissance philosophy —and from Lorenzo's brilliant circle of acquaintances; from Michelangelo's admiration for the fervor of Savonarola; via the traditional religious views of the Vatican under two very different popes; and from the passionate religious beliefs of Vittoria Colonna.

Michelangelo lived for almost 89 years—an unusually long life span for a man of his era. In 1557 he had been forced to leave Rome because of the threat of invasion by Spain; he spent several of the last years of his life traveling in much the same way as he had started his adult years. He returned to Rome after the threat had passed and it was there that his life ended; he was buried at the church of Saint Apostoli in a huge formal ceremony. However, the story of his remarkable life was not over even in death: after burial, his body was secretly reclaimed and smuggled back to Florence, on the orders of Duke Cosimo de' Medici. There it was laid to rest in the church of Santa Croce. It remains there today, in a magnificent marble tomb designed by Vasari in 1570. The tomb bears a bust of Michelangelo, below which are sculptures of three sorrowing women: *Architecture*, *Painting*, and *Sculpture*.

LUCINDA HAWKSLEY

COPY OF THE SAGRA DEL CARMINE (C. 1490)
Celimage.sa/Scala Archives

*T*HIS was Michelangelo's copy of Masaccio's *Sagra del Carmine*. Michelangelo's version is dated to around 1490 and is one of his earliest sketches. The copy shows a draped figure; the folds of his attire are formed with a careful crosshatching technique.

Florence, the undoubted nursery of the Renaissance, was the starting point for the genius, and would characterize Michelangelo. As a boy in this city Michelangelo was influenced by the works of the old masters, including frescoes by Masaccio and Giotto, of which he made several copies to develop his skills. Against his father's wishes, Michelangelo started an apprenticeship at the studio of Ghirlandaio. After one year he left Ghirlandaio in order to specialize in sculpture.

The quality of Michelangelo's draftsmanship was very high, considering his youth. His cross-hatching technique, especially in the forms and spaces of the drapery, is notable. A number of Michelangelo's early surviving works (he is known to have destroyed many such drawings) are copies based on earlier Italian masters such as Giotto or Masaccio. Others are drawn from ancient statuary.

Michelangelo went on to study at the sculpture school in the Medici gardens at Florence. There he attracted the patronage of Lorenzo de' Medici, the Magnificent.

TWO FIGURES AFTER GIOTTO (1490)
Celimage.sa/Scala Archives

IN 1488 Michelangelo was apprenticed for a term of three years to Domenico Ghirlandaio and must have learnt the elements of fresco technique from his master. After the death of the young artist's patron Lorenzo de' Medici in 1492 the political situation in Florence deteriorated, and in October 1494, Michelangelo left for Bologna. Here, he carved three small figures for the tomb of Sa. This figure is part of the whole extraordinary series of the Madonna and Child, with the different variations of Michelangelo's constant meditation on that great theme. The subject is always part of the salvation process. Here it functions specifically as the crucial point of the Resurrection.

Giotto's 1320 fresco at the Peruzzi Chapel in Santa Croce, Florence, has two figures at the left of the painting. These two figures are reproduced in a Michelangelo drawing of 1490, now held at the Louvre, Paris.

Reflecting the poses in Giotto's work, these figures are shown as supplicants at the adoration. They carry themselves with the patrician demeanor of a Florentine noble and his compatriot. Their robes are thick and heavy. Yet despite their obvious power there is a humility discernible in their expressions. This piece is an excellent example of the work of the young and very talented Michelangelo during the period of his apprenticeship.

MADONNA OF THE STEPS (1491–92)

Celimage.sa / Scala Archives

MADONNA *of the Steps* dates from 1491–92, during the period of Michelangelo's apprenticeship to the Florentine sculptor Bertoldo di Giovanni (*c.* 1420–91) at the Medici Palace. At that time the head of the Medici family was Lorenzo the Magnificent, the most powerful and influential man in Florence, an important patron of the arts and leader of the Renaissance. His vast collection of ancient sculpture and artefacts was housed in the garden of San Marco, a nearby monastery. Michelangelo had unlimited access to this treasure trove of antiquities and the influence of his studies there is apparent in this piece.

For this marble rectangular relief, Michelangelo has chosen the popular religious scene of the Madonna with the baby Jesus, to which he would return in later years with his sculpture *Madonna and Child* (1520–34). He departed from the traditional treatment of this theme by placing the Madonna sideways, a position often used in ancient Greek funerary decorations, which gives the piece a somber air.

The strong influence of Donatello (*c.* 1386–1466) is evident in the shallow pale-yellow marble relief, and although there are several faults in perspective, as well as in form, the work is representative of the development of an incredible talent in the young Michelangelo.

BATTLE OF HERCULES WITH THE CENTAURS (1491–92)
Celimage.sa/Scala Archives

ALONG with *Madonna of the Steps* (1491–92), the marble relief of *Battle of Hercules with the Centaurs* is counted among Michelangelo's earliest surviving pieces. Thought to have been started in 1491–92, but never completed, the piece presents a theme that was to dominate Michelangelo's work throughout his career—the male nude in movement. Here, as with his later cartoon *Battle of Cascina* (1504), Michelangelo created a consolidated expanse of male nudes frozen in a violent and turbulent struggle. Arms grab, push, or throw punches and both pieces focus on the men's interlocking limbs and the gestures forming this compact mass. Some of the figures are in relief while others, in the foreground of the sculpture, appear to be almost freestanding.

The theme of *Battle of Hercules with the Centaurs* was a popular choice in Classical sculpture, and the artist found inspiration for the work amongst the artefacts kept in the Medici garden. The piece is based on a tale in Ovid's (43 BC –18 AD) *Metamorphoses*, in which a wedding feast is disrupted by centaurs attempting to kidnap the women present, including the bride. Michelangelo has depicted all the figures as human, despite the centaurian subject of the relief, focusing mainly upon the muscular torsos of the men.

BACCHUS (C. 1496–97)
Celimage.sa/Lessing Archive

BACCHUS in Greek and Roman mythology was the god of the vine, wine, and mystic ecstasy, and Michelangelo chose to represent the two former qualities of the god. Bacchus, his head crowned with grapevines, stands with his cup held aloft as if about to offer a toast. His expression is one of vague puzzlement, as though he has forgotten what he intended to do. His head is tilted and his mouth open, while his eyes appear glazed and unfocused. The unsteady stance of the god furthers his drunken appearance; one leg is partly lifted while his body tilts backward, making him seem unsure of his footing, almost staggering in his drunken stupor.

The piece was commissioned by wealthy Roman banker Jacopo Galli between 1497–98, while Michelangelo was living in Rome. The piece was placed in his garden and at one point the raised arm was broken off deliberately to increase the statue's Classical appearance. *Bacchus* is the earliest surviving life-size statue by Michelangelo. The perfection of the natural, realistic form that Michelangelo achieved here shows, as does *David* (1501–04), that despite his youth, he was far beyond the reach and ability of other sculptors of his time.

SATYR (DETAIL FROM BACCHUS)
(C. 1496–97)
Celimage.sa/Lessing Archive

*I*N Classical mythology the satyr was a demon of nature, representing the animal elements of humanity with its half-man and half-animal form. The satyr was sometimes represented as a horse, but more commonly as having the legs and hindquarters of a goat, cloven hoofs, and budding horns. Traditionally satyrs were the attendants of Bacchus, following him around and joining in with his festivities and sybaritic excesses.

This diminutive satyr hides behind the back of Bacchus, who is swaying drunkenly, and he nibbles at the grapes he steals from the leopard skin that Bacchus holds loosely. It was with this statue, and in particular along the edges of limbs such as the satyr's leg, that Michelangelo started to perfect his use of the drill to create textured surfaces. This effect would not have been possible with his preferred tools—the claw, toothed, and flat chisels.

Bacchus was created to be viewed from every angle; to be a freestanding statue. When viewed from the front, the satyr can only be partially glimpsed and it is necessary to walk around the statue to see it fully. The two figures are not attached by their bodies but by the leopard skin and the grapes; the satyr's body, however, curves suggestively, mirroring the form of Bacchus.

PIETÀ, ST PETER'S (1498–99)
Celimage.sa/Scala Archives

*P*IETÀ (1497–99) established Michelangelo as a master sculptor beyond comparison with any of his contemporaries. The sculpture now stands in St Peter's, on a high pedestal and protected by bulletproof glass, following a recent attack.

The pietà, a scene in which the Virgin Mary supports the dead body of Jesus in her lap, was a popular subject matter in other areas of Europe but had rarely been depicted in Italy. The composition of the pietà had caused other artists much difficulty in creating a realistic position that allowed Mary to support the body of an adult man. Michelangelo solved this problem by making Mary's robes heavy and large, creating an area in which the body of Christ could lie across her lap.

Pietà shows a reversal of the popular theme of Madonna with Child that Michelangelo explored in his early work *Madonna of the Steps* (1491–92). In *Pietà*, Mary holds the lifeless body of her only son, her left hand stretched palm upward, as if she is questioning the fate of Jesus. This gesture draws the viewer in to the scene emphatically, reiterating the Christian belief that Jesus died for humanity's salvation.

29

THE VIRGIN'S HEAD
(DETAIL FROM PIETÀ) (1498–99)
Celimage.sa/Scala Archives

*D*URING Michelangelo's lifetime, the face of the Virgin in this statue was criticized for appearing too young to be that of the mother of the adult Christ. Michelangelo defended his creation by saying: "Don't you know that women who are chaste remain much fresher than those who are not? How much more so a virgin who was never touched by even the slightest lascivious desire ..." He went on to add that he portrayed Jesus as older to emphasize his humanity; that He had subjected himself to the effects of mortality.

"Pietà" is the Italian word for pity. Despite its youthful appearance, the face of Mary still manages to convey the tragedy of the scene. Her eyes are downcast, almost shut. There is a quiet stillness in her expression, as if she is accepting of the death of her son.

Across Mary's chest is a sash upon which Michelangelo carved the words "Michaelangelo Buonarroti Florentine made this." *Pietà* was the only work Michelangelo signed in this manner, and his biographers recorded that he overheard some people credit *Pietà* to another artist, so that night he carved his name across the piece. The manner in which the sash follows the shape of Mary's body underneath the drapes would indicate that this story is fiction. Nonetheless, the prominent positioning of his signature is evidence of Michelangelo's pride in his work.

DAVID (1501–04)
Celimage.sa/Lessing Archive

MICHELANGELO'S *David* (1501–04) sealed his reputation as the greatest living sculptor of the time. The piece was commissioned by Piero Soderini, the first chancellor of the Florentine republic, after the sculptor returned to Florence flushed with success from Rome.

The marble for *David* was a huge block that Renaissance sculptor Agostino di Duccio had abandoned about 40 years previously, and it had been lying disused ever since. Several other sculptors wanted the commission but Michelangelo was the only one to achieve a design of such enormous dimensions that used only this marble block, requiring no additional parts. Owing to the limitations of the damaged marble from which Michelangelo worked, the statue is much broader than it is deep, and so *David* was intended to be viewed from the front or back rather than the side.

For the Florentines, the Biblical character of David was an exemplar of strength and enormous courage in the face of adversity. Upon its completion the statue became a centerpiece of civic pride in the city, and Michelangelo would later draw upon this victory scene in the Sistine Chapel. His portrayal of David differs from other versions in form as well as in position—he uses developed, more muscular forms and creates a powerful physical presence in the spirit of a giant-slaying hero and future king.

FACE (DETAIL FROM DAVID) (1501–04)
Celimage.sa/Scala Archives

*A*S the Republicans had beaten the Medici family to gain ruling power in Florence, the subject of David was chosen as a reminder to the republican government that David had beaten mighty Goliath and that he had ruled his people well and fairly thereafter. The face of *David* emphasizes this idea through its watchful and expectant expression, frowning with intense concentration. This expression is matched by the almost stationary pose; he seems pensive yet alert with the loaded slingshot held lightly over one shoulder as he gazes into the distance, waiting for his foe to come within range.

Some critics have noted that the head and hands of *David* are slightly too large for the body. Given that the statue is almost 17 ft high, only photographs enable us to have a direct view of the youth's face, an experience not possible for a contemporary viewer. The model for the statue was an adolescent boy and these slightly over-defined features ring true in their natural rendering of a boy not quite fully grown.

The face itself is classically ideal, with perfect features. Upon completion of *David*, Piero Soderini told Michelangelo that the nose was too large. To appease him the sculptor climbed up the statue and carefully pretended to chisel at the nose, letting some marble dust fall to the ground to enforce his deceit.

THE DONI TONDO
(THE HOLY FAMILY) (1504)
Celimage.sa/Lessing Archive

*T*HE *Holy Family* is known as the *Doni Tondo*, since it was commissioned by Michelangelo's friend Angelo Doni in 1503–04. Michelangelo rarely worked in the medium of panel painting and the *Doni Tondo* is the only piece that can undeniably be attributed to him; other surviving paintings, such as *The Entombment* (c. 1506), have a more questionable status.

The three figures are closely linked together by their positions and their movements, forming a compact, almost sculptural whole. The round frame is set off by the triangular configuration and the delineation of the figures is crisp, almost harsh, with a sharp, clear definition. This is a technique that, while necessary in tempera painting, further increases the sculptural quality of the figures by making the three stand out against the background, as if they have been superimposed.

The colors are bold and brightly vivid; the orange-gold material of Joseph's clothes seems to have a satin sheen. Michelangelo used color in a similar way throughout the Sistine Chapel frescoes, as can be seen in *The Delphic Sibyl* (1508–12). The contrasting colors also create blocks within the figures that emphasize their movements.

ST JOHN THE BAPTIST
(DETAIL FROM THE HOLY FAMILY) (1504)
Celimage.sa/Lessing Archive

S T John the Baptist appears in the middle ground of the *Doni Tondo*, as he does in the later *Pitti Tondo* (c. 1504). With his animal skin draped round him, he gazes adoringly at the baby Jesus held aloft, symbolically, between his parents. A celestial light that seems to emanate from the family itself falls onto St John.

The distant landscape is barren, with a rocky mountain that can be seen at the top of this detail. Between the family and the mountains are five young male nudes. One of the nudes has his arm around the youth in front of him, while to their right another playfully tries to pull off the cloth that is draped over him. The significance of these nudes has been generally taken to be that they denote the pagan world from which St John has turned away to face the Holy Family, as if he can already sense their importance. Michelangelo created symbolic layers within this picture, representing the path of man: from the harsh natural world, to his naked paganism, to the intermediary St John, and to the Christian world, newly formed and represented by the child in the foreground.

STUDY FOR THE DONI MADONNA (1503)

Celimage.sa / Scala Archives

*M*ADONNA *and Child* (*Study for the Doni Tondo Madonna*) is a preliminary drawing for the *Doni Tondo* (1504). Michelangelo chose not to use the positioning seen here, opting for a triangular configuration. Michelangelo's preferred medium for this type of work was red chalk, which had been introduced by Leonardo da Vinci (1452–1519) during the year this work was executed. His confident depiction of the child demonstrates the ease with which he mastered new media, and he went on to use it frequently, as in his Study of Adam (1511).

From 1503, both Leonardo and Michelangelo were living in Florence. The two great artists were both later to receive a commission for battle scenes which were to be placed next to each other. There is said to have been great rivalry between the two; Leonardo had long been acknowledged as a genius, while Michelangelo was still building his reputation, although his success with *Pietà* and *Bacchus* had considerably strengthened his fame. Michelangelo also derived the notion of a triangular configuration—which he used for the Holy Family in his *Doni Tondo*—from Leonardo's work, but it was an idea that he developed and made his own.

ST PETER (1501–04)
Celimage.sa/Scala Archives

ST *Peter* is one of several statues of saints that Michelangelo made for the Cardinal Francesco Piccolomini. Piccolomini went on to become Pope Pius III in 1503 but died after only three weeks. On Michelangelo's return to Florence in 1501, flushed with the success of his *Pietà* in Rome, he received a three-year commission from the future Pope to carve 15 statues of saints. Each statue was to be 4.5 ft high and they were to be situated in the Piccolomini altar in Siena Cathedral. Following the death of the Pope, the contract was renewed by his heirs, but Michelangelo was never to fulfill its terms, delivering only four of the saints in 1504—*St Peter, St Pius, St Paul,* and *St Gregory*.

    St Peter leans slightly to one side with his knee bent and raised, giving the appearance of being caught in mid-step. His head is lowered, his eyes humbly kept to the ground. The statue is a conventional treatment of the saint, unlike the St Peter seen in the fresco of *The Crucifixion of St Peter.*

THE MADONNA OF BRUGES (1501–04)
Celimage.sa/Lessing Archive

SET within the decorative high altar of the richly decorated Church of Our Lady of Notre Dame in Bruges, Belgium, this masterpiece is an extraordinary and reverential work. Also known as the *Bruges Madonna*, this statue was carved by Michelangelo at about the same time that he was working on the colossal statue of David. During the same time period Michelangelo produced several Madonna paintings and sculptures, including the painting of the Holy Family known as the *Doni Madonna*. From about 1505 onward Michelangelo devoted nearly all of his time to large-scale projects.

This work focuses on the seated Madonna, who has the nude Christ Child standing between her knees. The Madonna figure has a haunting and ethereal beauty. The richly detailed folds of her drapery lend an astonishing realism to this High Renaissance work.

THE PITTI TONDO (C. 1504)
Courtesy of Edimedia

*T*HE *Pitti Tondo* (1504–05) and the *Taddei Tondo* (c. 1504) were named after the Florentine families that commissioned them. By the time these two marble reliefs were made, Michelangelo was a very famous artist and his work was highly sought after. Both of these pieces were left unfinished, and it has been suggested that this is because Michelangelo returned to Rome in 1505. Others believe, however, that he left them in this state deliberately; the Pitti Tondo appears to be a finished work in which Michelangelo quite consciously used the effects of the unfinished surfaces as an aesthetic device.

"Tondo" means a round framed picture or relief. The *Pitti Tondo* was one of three tondi Michelangelo worked on in the space of two years, seeking different ways to make use of circular space. Here Michelangelo has broken the constraints of the circle by placing Mary's head outside it. To the left of Mary is the vague figure of St John, who also appears in the other tondi.

The *Pitti Tondo* relief is less deep than that of the *Taddei Tondo*. To create the illusion of perspective in the placement of St John, the relief is very shallow; he is ghost-like, being only lightly defined.

STUDY FOR THE BATTLE OF CASCINA (1504)
Celimage.sa / Scala Archives

*I*N 1504 Piero Soderini commissioned Michelangelo to create a huge fresco depicting a battle scene. This was to be placed in the Signoria Palace alongside *The Battle of Anghiari*, to be produced by Leonardo da Vinci. Michelangelo's invitation to the Vatican by Pope Julius II meant that the painting was never executed, although several studies survive.

The fresco shows the story of a surprise attack by Pisan forces on the Florentine army, who were caught unawares whilst bathing in the river Arno. In *Study for The Battle of Cascina* we can discern a group of writhing figures, a mixture of vanquished victims and desperate survivors.

The study is a seminal example of Michelangelo's evolving style and contains clear examples of the artist's rigid, sculptural approach to figurative subjects. Through examination of his epic drawings, such as *Study for The Battle of Cascina*, we begin to comprehend the processes that led to his large-scale paintings. We can discern the internal dynamism of the overall work, which belies its softly etched tones.

STUDY FOR A FIGURE FROM THE
BATTLE OF CASCINA (1504)
Celimage.sa / Scala Archives

*T*HE *Battle of Cascina* cartoon was highly influential, and studied by many contemporary artists who visited Florence. Several effusive descriptions of the cartoon exist from renowned artists such as Benvenuto Cellini (1500–71). Many claimed that the cartoon was superior even to Michelangelo's painting of the Sistine Chapel.

The cartoon's significance stems not just from the influence it exerted but also from its signaling the development of Michelangelo's exclusive focus on the male nude in motion. The story of the Florentine captain raising alarm among his soldiers bathing in the river Arno provided an excellent opportunity to explore the many postures and poses of the body and gave a pretext for nudity. As in all his work the background is simple, the intensity of his focus directed purely on the human form.

This study shows the superb naturalism of the muscles working in the youth's back and gives an idea of what the original cartoon must have been like in the hands of the master. Bastiano da Sangallo's work often presents an anatomically inaccurate portrayal of the human body; this is evident when comparing Michelangelo's study with the same figure at the top of the da Sangallo cartoon.

ST MATTHEW (1505)
Celimage.sa / Scala Archives

*T*HE Florentine Wool Guild and the Opera del Duomo commissioned Michelangelo to carve 12 statues of the apostles for Florence Cathedral in 1503. The Guilds were important patrons of the arts and the commission was a prestigious one for Michelangelo. Patronage of the arts had developed alongside the increase in wealth within the city and in turn had greatly improved the standing of the artist in society.

It was agreed that Michelangelo would produce one apostle statue a year, but *St Matthew* was the only piece that Michelangelo had begun. By the end of 1505, following his return to Rome, the contract was canceled before his work was completed.

The statue of *St Matthew* is significant, since it indicates the emergence of an important stage in Michelangelo's career; the study of the body in contorted movement. The figure has one smooth, almost completed knee raised while his opposite arm grips the side of the huge marble block, as if he were about to push himself up and out of the marble constraint. Michelangelo was to continue exploring this new area of movement in his frescoes in the Sistine Chapel, especially the *Ignudi* (1508–12).

MALE NUDE (FULL FACING) (1502–06)
Celimage.sa/Lessing Archive

*T*HE *Male Nude* uses a medium of red chalk, often employed by Michelangelo as it was softer than black chalk. The artist has drawn the sketch with great attention to detail, yet it appears uncompleted. Michelangelo emphasized the torso, arms, and legs, leaving the head vague and ill-defined.

Through foreshortening, the artist has effectively established mobility and perspective within this figure. Muscle shape and shaded areas create the realistic illusion of the leg and body in motion. This is a preparatory study for a full-scale work. There is no suggestion of context or background.

Male Nude's posture is dramatic and extreme. Michelangelo's use of such postures influenced the art style known as Mannerism (*c.* 1515–1610), which employed artistic tricks such as elongating a figure to heighten its dramatic impact.

TWO NUDE MEN RAISING A THIRD MAN
(1502–06)
Celimage.sa/Lessing Archive

MICHELANGELO has been quoted as saying that an "artist must have his measuring tools, not in the hand, but in the eye, because the hands do but operate, it is the eye that judges...." He was a superb draftsman, a skill that he believed was paramount to all the arts in which he excelled, whether it was sculpture, painting, or architecture.

Two Nude Men Raising a Third Man shows the artist's skill at handling the human figure in movement. The men's torsos appear to be pushing forward out of the frame, half staggering toward the viewer. The absence of facial features adds to this rough quality, as does the balancing of the body and the arm thrust up from the central figure. The men are thickset, muscular, and reminiscent of representations of figures that appear in Michelangelo's later paintings. The heavier forms that filled his final works have been described as evidence of his disillusionment with the portrayal of the perfect male form, once so prevalent in his sculpture, painting, and drawings. There is the suggestion of a struggle to achieve a goal in which the three men are playing an interdependent role.

THE VIRGIN, ST ANNE, AND MALE NUDE

THE VIRGIN, ST ANNE, AND MALE NUDE (1502–06)
Celimage.sa/Lessing Archive

*T*HIS work, embellished with quotes from Petrarch, is a finely detailed rendition of two biblical figures. The additional male figure appears as a footnote to the main portrait.

This is an especially penetrative portrayal. We are reminded of Leonardo da Vinci's work *Virgin, Infant, and St Anne*, which offers a more empathetic treatment of the subject. The two artists shared similar family backgrounds and early childhood experiences.

Michelangelo (1475–1564) was born in Tuscany, Italy, and was raised by a wet nurse until the age of two, because his mother was ill. His mother died when he was six, and his father remarried. His childhood is usually described as lacking affection, and he retained a grim and taciturn demeanor throughout his life.

Leonardo (1452–1519) was also born in Tuscany, the illegitimate son of a wealthy notary and a peasant woman. His father took custody of the boy, and each of Leonardo's parents married other people, eventually providing him with 17 half-sisters and half-brothers. Leonardo's first stepmother died when he was 12, and his second stepmother died when he was 21.

Perhaps fueled by their early loss of a strong maternal figure, the art of both men is infused with a wish to reunite with the mother, and these "conflicts of masculine and feminine forces show in the sublime genius of their art," according to the distinguished art historian, Dr Simons.

Like Leonardo, Michelangelo crafted many renditions of the Virgin Mary and her mother, St Anne, many of them depicting mother figures who are aloof.

DIFFERENT STUDIES OF FIGURES, WITH AN INSCRIPTION AFTER A SONNET BY PETRARCH (1506)
Celimage.sa/Lessing Archive

*F*RANCIS Petrarch (Francesco Petrarca) was born in Arezzo, the son of a notary, but he spent his early childhood in a village near Florence. The Black Guelfs, who had seized power in Florence, expelled his father, Ser Petracco. In Avignon Petrarch composed numerous popular sonnets. In his search for old Latin classics and manuscripts, he traveled through France, Germany, Italy, and Spain.

Petrarch was regarded as the greatest scholar of his age. He wrote most of his works in Latin, although his sonnets and *canzoni*, written in Italian, were equally influential. Petrarch was known as a devoted student of antiquity. He combined an interest in classical culture with Christianity and had a deep influence on literature throughout western Europe.

In *Different Studies of Figures*, Michelangelo demonstrates his abiding deference to classical form in art. In this ink sketch he combines several anatomical and figurative elements. The arm set to the foreground establishes a distance behind which a tall androgynous figure stands. Other elements such as the helmeted head appear as visual references in the form of an *aide-mémoire* for the artist who is perhaps making quick notes for some future work.

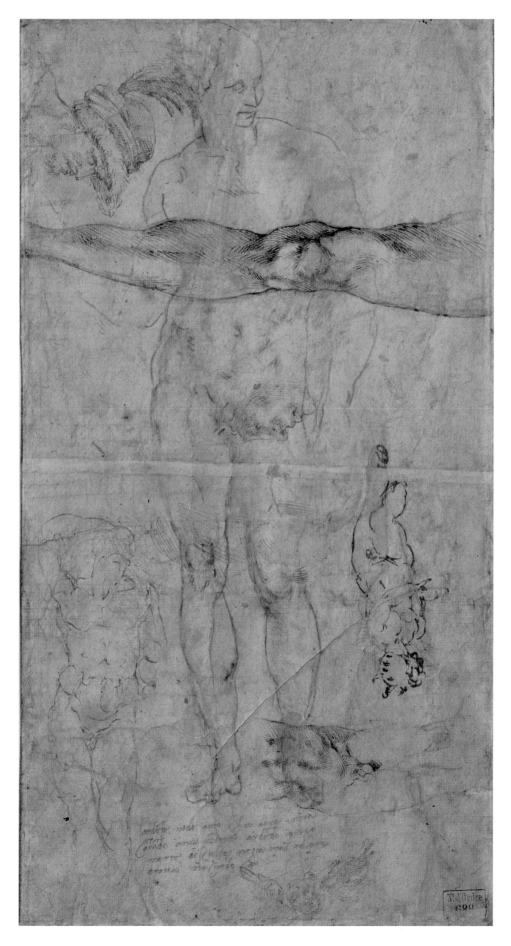

THE SEPARATION OF LIGHT FROM DARKNESS (1508–12)
Celimage.sa/Scala Archives

*C*HRONOLOGICALLY the first panel in the narrative scheme, *The Separation of Light from Darkness* is seen last if entering the Sistine Chapel through the lay entrance. Michelangelo chose to begin painting here and worked back toward the altar wall. The first five panels depict the creations of God, beginning here with the *Creation of Form from Chaos (Separation of Light from Darkness)*. The narrative then moves on to highlight the Biblical history of mankind, starting with *The Fall of Man*, followed by three panels that show stories of *Noah and The Flood*. The narrative panels end with a panel that alludes to the re-emergence of sin amongst mankind, thus announcing the coming of Christ which links the panels to the earlier frescoes within the chapel.

Michelangelo was the first artist to attempt the illustration of such an ethereal and intangible subject as the beginning of the universe and he chose a literal translation of the Bible, focusing solely on the recognizable: the figure of God. God fills almost the entire panel as he reaches ahead, the appearance of movement created by the swirling colors about him.

THE CREATION OF ADAM (1508–12)
Celimage.sa/Lessing Archive

*T*HE notion of God creating Man had been represented in art before Michelangelo began working on the Sistine Chapel, but never with the majesty and vitality that he achieved. This treatment is not reserved purely for the figure of God but is equally abundant in Adam, fittingly so for a being made in God's image. Adam has been painted nude, a massive figure reclining against a rocky mountain amid an otherwise barren landscape. He is gracefully poised, a perfection of form—muscular yet beautifully proportioned—a heroically Classical image.

God is shown in movement, as He is in the preceding three panels, which portray images of Creation. The gestures and expressions of the angels and cherubs clinging to His side emphasize His movement; some are watching expectantly as the two hands draw close.

The scale within *The Creation of Adam* is larger than in the preceding panels. The scaffolding had been removed from the completed half of the ceiling by this time and upon viewing it, Michelangelo decided to increase the size of the figures and decrease the detail, making the paintings more impressive and startling to the audience below.

THE HAND OF GOD
(DETAIL FROM THE CREATION OF ADAM)
(1508–12)

Celimage.sa/Lessing Archive

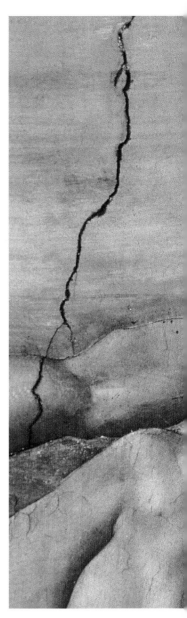

*T*HE *Hand of God* is perhaps the most enduring of Michelangelo's paintings. Almost five centuries later this image remains prevalent and is still being used in advertising and on posters and T-shirts. This is particularly true of the detail that shows the two hands as they reach toward each other, tantalizingly close, almost touching.

The panel illustrates the moment when life is instilled in Adam by God. Michelangelo has placed the central focus upon the hands of God and of Adam, not just by the placement of the figures, but also by the lines of form that flow within the painting between the two outstretched arms.

Adam, who is only half sitting up against the mountainside, seems weak and languid, with his arm resting upon one bent knee as if it is too heavy for him to hold up without some support. The hand is limp, the fingers are drooping as if they are without energy, awaiting the vital spark of life.

THE CREATION OF EVE AND THE
PROPHET EZEKIEL (1508–1512)
Celimage.sa / Lessing Archive

MICHELANGELO painted a complex architectural structure, resembling that used for the tomb of Pope Julius II, to give his mammoth fresco structural order. The panel of *The Creation of Eve* is blocked off by two of the 10 painted pilasters that separate the huge ceiling into the nine sections used for the central narrative panels. On either side of the small panel are two of the four larger narrative panels.

Figures of naked men perch at the base of the pilasters, and they are often shown twisted in movement, demonstrating Michelangelo's skill at handling the male nude. Pairs of these figures, known as *Ignudi*, appear at either side of the smaller panels and hold medallions between them containing scenes from Biblical history.

Underneath the *Ignudi*, carved into the columns, are small cherubic figures, also known as caryatids, who appear to prop up the cornice above them. Darkly painted nudes appear besides the caryatids in the triangular spaces created by the spandrels, beneath the larger narrative panels. They seem crammed into their tiny spaces, pushing against their confinement. Underneath the medallion that the *Ignudi* hold sits the prophet Ezekiel.

THE FALL OF MAN AND THE EXPULSION
FROM PARADISE (1508–12)
Celimage.sa/Lessing Archive

MICHELANGELO used the same device of continuous narrative for this large panel of *The Fall of Man and the Expulsion from Paradise* that he used in *The Creation of the Planets, the Sun, and the Moon.* The tale begins on the left, with the figure of Adam grabbing the branches of a tree while Eve sits beneath him. Eve reaches behind her to take the apple from the serpent, while Adam stretches to grasp one of the forbidden fruits. The narrative continues its flow through the serpent in the tree on to the right, where the couple can be seen as they are cast out of Paradise.

The landscape is barren, almost inhospitable, with only a few rocks surrounding the figures, with the exception of the one tree where the serpent lurks. This is an unusual depiction of Paradise, contrasting with the verdant foliage and lush vegetation that can be seen in traditional representations of the story, or even in the fifteenth-century frescoes that line the second tier of the Sistine chapel.

Throughout the work there is a noticeable lack of detailed background or landscapes; Michelangelo's priority was always the natural and realistic depiction of the human form.

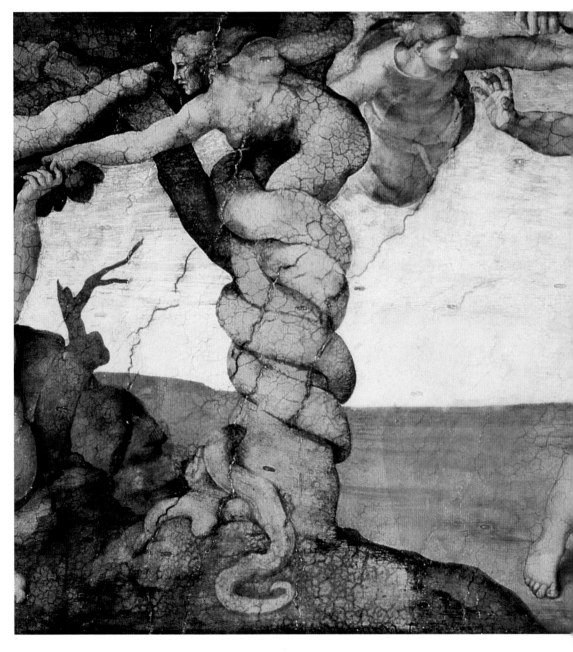

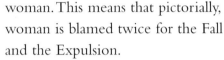

THE SNAKE AND THE EXPULSION
(DETAIL FROM THE FALL OF MAN) (1508–12)
Celimage.sa/Lessing Archive

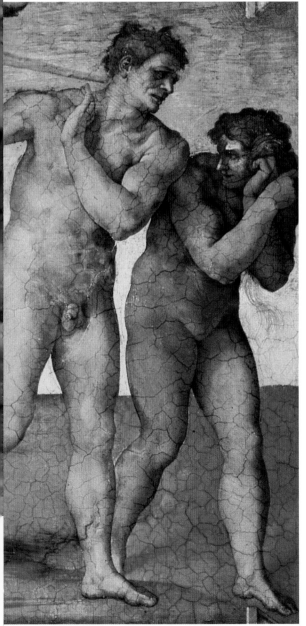

THE snake from the Garden of Eden is usually portrayed as male or genderless. Michelangelo chose a feminine depiction for his serpent, tempting the eagerly awaiting Eve with the forbidden fruit while also focusing her gaze on the nearby Adam. Her lower half, in the form of a snake, is painted in lurid, bright colors whilst her top half takes the form of a voluptuous and tempting woman. This means that pictorially, woman is blamed twice for the Fall and the Expulsion.

On the right of the fresco, Adam and Eve are shown leaving Eden. Adam looks away from the scene of their disgrace, his hands sheltering his eyes from the sight as they are pushed out of their paradise by the angel hovering above. Eve looks back, her body hunched forward with her hand against her face as if trying to hide herself in shame. There are interesting comparisons to be drawn between Adam's tortured body and the majestic figure in *The Creation of Adam. The Expulsion* leans heavily on Masaccio's famous *Expulsion from Paradise*, in the Brancacci Chapel in Florence, a piece with which Michelangelo was certainly familiar.

THE FLOOD (1508–12)
Celimage.sa/Lessing Archive

BELIEVED to have been the first narrative panel that
Michelangelo painted, *The Flood* offers a wealth of images
crowded together. It is the smallest of the nine panels and
when viewed from the floor of the chapel it is difficult to make out
the finer points of the piece. It is thought that he changed the scale
after seeing *The Flood* from the ground, as all the subsequent panels
have larger and fewer figures.

Given the similarities in their subject matter,
The Flood bears a great resemblance to the later fresco,
The Last Judgment, with its mass of troubled bodies. In the
foreground of the picture, a woman lies despondent on
the hillside. Behind her a long line of people, some
bearing children, women or belongings, struggle up the
hill, in an attempt to gain sanctuary from the rising water.
One figure clings frantically to a tree, bent almost double
in the wind. To the right, a man carries the lifeless body of
another toward a tent full of huddled people, who reach
out their arms to help him. This compassionate portrayal
dissolves in the background, where figures can be seen
beating one another on the boat, and again on the ark.

IGNUDI BETWEEN THE DRUNKENNESS OF NOAH AND THE FLOOD (1508–12)

Celimage.sa/Scala Archives

*A*MONG the many nude figures that can be seen within and upon the painted architectural frame of the fresco, there are 20 *Ignudi,* placed in pairs on either side of the small narrative panels. They share delicate, almost feminine facial features and active figures. Their symbolism, or whether they actually have any, has been greatly debated and many theories for their inclusion in the ceiling have been expressed. Some believe that the *Ignudi* represent the ideal of man; others argue that they represent ancient pagan societies.

The first two sets of *Ignudi* to be painted surround *The Drunkenness of Noah.* For these first two pairs, Michelangelo used a cartoon for one of the *Ignudi* and then reversed it for the *Ignudo* placed opposite, so that they acted as mirrors to each other; the only difference between the paired *Ignudi* was to be in tone and minor details. This technique was quickly abandoned, however. It was initially devised in order that Michelangelo could pass on work to assistants, but he soon became dissatisfied with their work and dismissed them, continuing to work alone. The subsequent *Ignudi* were individually drawn.

IGNUDO NEAR THE SACRIFICE OF NOAH
Celimage.sa / Scala Archives

MOVING along the ceiling from *The Drunkenness of Noah* through to *The Separation of Light from Darkness*, the *Ignudi* take on various extreme postures, becoming increasingly animated. This *Ignudo*, with his arm thrown across his face, seems to be trying to hide his eyes from the sight of the events taking place in the panel above him. He is precariously placed on the edge of his pedestal and his torso leans forward and to the right, as if he is trying to escape. The panel is *The Sacrifice of Noah*, and Noah's son is seen holding a bundle of wood.

The placement of the *Ignudi* beneath the four corners of the panels, and their frontal positioning, draws the viewer's eye into the narrative panel. The expressions of fear or agitation that some of the *Ignudi* have adds to this, causing the viewer to wonder what it is they are pulling away from.

Once again, this *Ignudo* recalls Michelangelo's love of contorted sculptural poses, as shown in the *Dying Slave* (1513–16), one of the sculptures he worked on for the *Tomb of Pope Julius II* (1505–43), before and after the Sistine Chapel.

IGNUDO BY THE DRUNKENNESS OF NOAH (1508–12)
Celimage.sa/Scala Archives

SITTING in a relaxed pose, the *Ignudo* leans back against the pilaster, one hand languidly holding on to the material that contains his medallion. The other *Ignudi* that surround *The Drunkenness of Noah* also share an air of despondency, with sad, downcast eyes, as if reflecting upon the event of mankind's return to sin that is depicted within the panel. The medallion, showing a scene from ancient Biblical history, has a piece missing and a crack that also runs through the *Ignudo*. The other *Ignudo* in this panel is missing; only his head and the calves remain following an explosion at the nearby Castel Sant'Angelo in 1797, which damaged the top left corner of *The Flood*.

This was not the first time *The Flood* had been damaged. Shortly after completing the panel Michelangelo was dismayed to find a fine mold growing from the plaster. He quoted the mold as evidence to the Pope that he knew too little of the techniques of fresco painting to complete the ceiling successfully. This attempt to get himself removed from the project was ignored: his mistake at leaving the plaster too damp was pointed out to him and he was commanded to continue in his work.

IGNUDO BY THE LIBYAN SIBYL (1508–12)
Celimage.sa/Scala Archives

AS well as serving to draw the viewer's eye into the panel, the *Ignudi* perform another important and practical purpose within the ceiling in camouflaging the increase in scale that occurs from the central narrative panels to the statuesque proportions of the prophets and sibyls. By placing these intermediary *Ignudi* between the prophets or sibyls and the narrative panels, Michelangelo has cleverly focused the viewer's attention away from the discontinuity in perspective that developed within the ceiling and onto the graceful figures of the *Ignudi*.

This *Ignudo* sits beneath the panel of *The Separation of Light from Darkness*, but he faces away from the events of the panel to look over his shoulder. His eyes are focused downward, nearly closed, onto the heads of the viewers beneath.

The rounded form and the feminine face of the *Ignudo* is reminiscent of the *Delphic Sibyl*, indeed it could almost be the mirror reflection of the sibyl's pose. It is possible that Michelangelo based this *Ignudo* on the same cartoon that he used for the *Delphic Sibyl*, merely reversing their position and decreasing the scale.

ANCESTOR OF CHRIST (1508–12)

Celimage.sa / Scala Archives

*T*HE arched windows of the chapel are on the upper tier of the building. A semicircular space, or lunette, is formed between each window arch and the top of the vaulted ceiling. The top of these lunettes forms the bottom of the spandrels (the top of one spandrel can be seen in the left corner of the detail), so it was fitting that the lunettes should share the same theme as the spandrels, which was the Ancestors of Christ.

The lunette ancestors share the same despondent, hopeless attitude that the spandrel ancestors portray; suggested mostly by their apathetic postures. In the lunettes, most of the ancestors of Christ appear alone, as opposed to the family groupings of the spandrels.

This old man seems both frail and weary. He has heavily rounded shoulders with a hunched back and leans on the stone with a hand and foot placed to steady himself. He is holding a staff, which suggests that he is a shepherd; a wind blows his beard out in front of him, giving an impression of harsh weather. The man rests one foot against the decorative plaster that surmounts the window in a gesture that continues the architectural conceit of the illusionary setting in the ceiling.

ESTHER AND HAMAN
(1508–12)
Celimage.sa/Scala Archives

ONE of four corner spandrels, *Esther and Haman* tells the story of Esther, the wife of a Persian king who denied her Jewish heritage until Haman, the king's minister, planned to slaughter all Jews. Esther appealed to her king on behalf of the Jews and Haman was subsequently hanged. The tale of Esther augurs Mary's pleading for mankind on Judgment Day, connecting this panel with the later fresco *The Last Judgment* (1536–41) positioned on the right.

Esther and Haman is another continual narrative: to the left of the scene Esther denounces Haman, to the right the king lies awake in bed. Next Haman is seen greeting Mordecai, whom he plots to have hanged. Finally, the central, dominant image of the piece is of the contorted figure of Haman being crucified.

Michelangelo has painted the figure of Haman as if he were running; the cross he is on is twisted so that his limbs are flung out and in front of his body rather than in the more usual side position, shown in *The Crucifixion of Christ* (c. 1541) on page 225. The suggestion of movement in the trapped body is symbolic of Haman's desperate struggle to free himself.

JUDITH CARRYING THE HEAD OF HOLOFERNES (1508–12)
Celimage.sa/Scala Archives

AT the corners of the ceiling are four spandrels which Michelangelo used to illustrate stories of the saviors of the Jews. In the two spandrels over the lay entrance of the chapel, near the final narrative panel *The Drunkenness of Noah*, Michelangelo painted two stories of the weak overcoming their rivals: *Judith and Holofernes* and *David and Goliath*.

This scene shows Judith making her escape after killing Holofernes, the leader of the attacking forces of the Assyrians, who were holding the Israelites under siege. In the center of the painting two women leave a bedchamber in which the body of a naked man lies, with his knees bent and torso stretching away from the viewer so that his neck cannot be seen. Judith looks at Holofernes' body as she lifts a sheet to cover the head that her maid carries in a tray.

The scene within the spandrel, and in *David and Goliath* opposite it, is relatively simple in form by comparison with the other two spandrels at the opposite end of the ceiling, such as *Esther and Haman*.

THE PERSIAN SIBYL (1508–12)

Celimage.sa/Lessing Archive

APPEARING at opposite sides of each of the five smaller narrative panels are the massive figures of the prophets and the sibyls. There are five sibyls and seven prophets overall, with two prophets at either end of the ceiling and the rest alternating with the sibyls. The sibyls sit on the opposite side of a panel to a prophet; the old *Persian Sibyl* sits opposite the young *Prophet Daniel*.

The sibyls were female prophets from ancient times, so their appearance here could seem at odds with the Christian theme of the ceiling. They were included because they foretold the coming of Christ and so are symbolic links between the ancient pagan civilizations and the Christian world. The inclusion of the sibyls also represented the non-Jewish tradition of oracles, ensuring that the ceiling was not dominated by Jewish symbols and stories such as the prophets.

The Persian sibyl is credited with the prophecy of the Virgin Mary conquering the Beast of the Apocalypse. Very little of her face can be seen as she turns away to study her predictions in the book she holds.

THE CUMAEAN SIBYL (1508–12)

Celimage.sa/Lessing Archive

*T*HE *Cumaean Sibyl* illustrates a failing of Michelangelo's that many critics have highlighted: although he was a master of the male nude, his skill at handling the female form was not parallel to this. In *The Creation of Eve* the figure of Eve seems bulky, servile and somewhat misshapen compared with the grace, poise and dignity of Adam in the preceding panel.

The *Cumaean Sibyl* shares this awkward portrayal; she has the heavily, muscular body of a man, with a head too small for her massive body. Her breasts, seen through the sheerness of her clothes, do not seem realistic for such a masculine frame. This inability of the artist to portray the female form may be attributed to his lack of knowledge of women: at the time it was hard to recruit female models for fear of their being regarded as prostitutes, so he used male models only. In addition, it is likely that he was homosexual; Michelangelo once opined in a poem that the grace of the male body was superior to that of the female. Despite the flaws, the *Cumaean Sibyl* is still an impressive figure as she leans over her book of prophecies, her face frowning with apprehension at what she foresees.

THE ERITHRAEAN SIBYL (1508–12)

Celimage.sa/Lessing Archive

*T*HE *Erithraean Sibyl*, placed beneath the narrative panel of
The Sacrifice of Noah, reiterates the fact that she was Noah's
daughter-in-law; it was she who foresaw the coming of
Judgment Day. As well as symbolizing the link between the ancient
Classical and Christian worlds, the sibyls also function as
representatives of the ancient civilizations from which they came:
Erithraea represents Ionia, Delphica Greece, Persica the Persian
Empire, Cumaea Rome and Libya the continent of Africa.

Erithraea sits with her legs crossed and her face toward that of
the neighboring prophet, Ezekiel. With one muscular arm, she reaches
forward to turn the pages of her book, whilst the other is relaxed by her
side. This posture leaves the upper half of her body in an open, frontal
position in contrast with the twisted, closed lower half of her body.

Above her book are two genii, one hidden in shadow. These
genii appear in pairs next to all of the prophets and sibyls. Their
significance is believed to be related to the neo-platonic philosophy
that every person is born with two such spirits that reflect the dual
nature of their spiritual and material sides. The genii blow upon the
flames of a torch to enable the sibyl to read her book.

ERITHRAEA

THE DELPHIC SIBYL (1508–12)
Celimage.sa/Lessing Archive

*T*HE Delphic sibyl foretold the coming of a great prophet who would be born to a virgin who knew nothing of the corruption of man. A wind is blowing over the prophetess; her hair trails out behind her and her cloak billows out round her shoulders. The hair of her two genii that stand behind her, mimicking her actions, also seems ruffled by this wind. This sense of the blowing wind together with the sibyl's wide-eyed and fearful expression, with her mouth ajar as she looks out past the viewer to see the future that approaches, gives the *Delphic Sibyl* a grave air of import.

Like the *Cumaean Sibyl*, the *Delphic Sibyl* is placed in a frontal position, while the other sibyls are all seen in varying degrees of a twisted, half-turned position. The *Delphic Sibyl* is a far more confident rendering of the female form: she has delicate, feminine features and a well-proportioned body.

Michelangelo used startling colors in the robes of the *Delphic Sibyl*, creating a vivid contrast of burnt orange and lime green.

THE PROPHET ZACHARIAH
Celimage.sa / Scala Archives

*T*HE prophets appear in the Old Testament. They are the inspired men of Israel, through whom the Holy Spirit tells of the coming of Christ and of the Christian era. Of the seven prophets that appear in the Sistine Chapel, four are major prophets and three are minor. *Zachariah* is one of the three minor prophets and is positioned at the end over the lay entrance to the chapel; at the altar end is the prophet *Jonah*. Zachariah had eight apocalyptical visions, one of which was of four chariots colored red, black, white, and piebald, that represented the four winds carrying God's judgment to the four corners of the earth. Zachariah also predicted the coming of the Messiah and the crucifixion.

Gold paint has been used on the decorations adorning the pilasters on either side of the prophets. Originally it was planned that there would be much more gilding within the ceiling fresco, but Michelangelo stopped painting following an argument with Pope Julius II. Julius wanted Michelangelo to carry out further gilding, saying that the fresco would look "poor" without it. Michelangelo replied that "those who are painted there were poor men," and so the gilding was left as it now stands.

THE PROPHET EZEKIEL (1508–12)
Celimage.sa/Scala Archives

*O*F all the prophets and sibyls, it is *Ezekiel* that is charged with the most energy and movement. A wind is apparent in the painting that blows the prophet's hair and robes, adding to his animated appearance. Clutching his scroll of prophecies in one hand, he twists in his seat, turning his head to one side as his massive body leans forward. One hand is held open in a gesture of questioning as he gazes with a severe intensity to his right. *Ezekiel* appears beneath the panel *The Creation of Eve*, opposite the *Cumaean Sibyl*, but he faces toward the *Erithraean Sibyl*. While the *Erithraean sibyl* foresaw the Judgment Day, in a vision Ezekiel saw the skeletal dead rising to assume flesh and clothing, which was interpreted as the resurrection of the dead on Judgment Day. Michelangelo later illustrated this vision in his *Last Judgment* fresco.

With his wild, gray beard and dominating presence, Ezekiel bears much resemblance to the figure of God as Michelangelo portrayed him in his narrative panels. The intense frown here is especially reminiscent of God's fierce expression in the panel *The Creation of the Planets, the Sun, and the Moon.*

THE PROPHET JOEL
Celimage.sa / Lessing Archive

JOEL is one of the 12 minor prophets. His predictions included the arrival of Judgment Day and a plague of locusts devouring the earth, blotting out the sun, moon, and the stars.

Michelangelo portrayed Joel as an old man: his face is lined, his expression serious and attentive as he reads from the scroll that he holds. The genius behind him on the left is mimicking his pose and also reading from the scroll with a solemn face. The other genius carries a book of prophecies while he points to the distance, his mouth open as if he himself is uttering a prophecy. The two nearest caryatids on the pilasters also turn to read the scroll that Joel carries.

Joel appears beneath the panel of *The Drunkenness of Noah* as well as opposite the *Delphic Sibyl*, and so was one of the first prophets to be painted. The increase in scale that Michelangelo employed in the later panels of the ceiling can also be seen in the prophets and sibyls. Joel sits in a simple, relaxed pose, easily fitting within the confines of his setting, whilst the later prophet Jeremiah leans forward out of his throne.

THE PROPHET DANIEL (1508–12)
Celimage.sa/Scala Archives

DANIEL is one of the four major prophets, along with Ezekiel, Isaiah and Jeremiah, and here represents Justice, one of the four cardinal virtues. During his lifetime, Daniel's prophetic gifts brought him much success and honor at the courts of kings. One of his most famous prophecies came from the interpretation of the writing that mysteriously appeared upon the walls during a feast at Belshazzar's court, the prediction of Belshazzar's death and the subsequent division of his kingdom. This incident has passed into everyday use with the saying "seen the writing on the wall."

Of all the prophets in the fresco, *Daniel* has been given the most youthful appearance and his pose and expression, like that of Ezekiel, suggests energy and movement. He leans forward from his throne, and the curve of the ceiling means that he appears to be looking down onto the chapel floor. He writes with one hand while holding his book of prophecies in the other. Placed between Daniel's legs is his genius, who bears the weight of the large book upon his head and shoulders. His other genius hides in shadow behind him, barely seen.

DANIEL

THE ANCESTORS OF CHRIST (DETAIL SHOWING DAVID AND GOLIATH) (1508–12)

Celimage.sa/Lessing Archive

BETWEEN each prophet and sibyl are the spandrels that Michelangelo filled with his illustrations of the Ancestors of Christ. Above each spandrel, leaning against the steeply sloping sides, are two figures. The symbolism of these figures is unclear. They are painted in deep golden or bronze colors and display a variety of complicated, dramatic poses. Most of the figures seem to be imprisoned within their niches, straining against the walls with their bodies. The niches in which they sit are shadowy and their features are difficult to see. It has been suggested that these dark, foreboding figures are intended to be representative of pre-Christian societies.

With their contorted positions and cramped attitudes these figures could also be reflective of the artist's working conditions in the Sistine Chapel. The ceiling fresco took over four years to complete, during which time Michelangelo spent many of his days in convoluted contortions upon the scaffolding. He made a joke of the physical trials that he had endured in a poem to a friend:

"My beard turns up to heaven; my nape falls in,
Fixed on my spine: my breast-bone visibly
Grows like a harp: a rich embroidery
Bedews my face from brush-drops thick and thin."

TOMB OF POPE JULIUS II (1505–45)

Celimage.sa/Scala Archives

ST Julius II, known as the Warrior Pope after his campaigns to reclaim lost papal states and fiefdoms, was a great patron of the arts. Julius wanted a suitably grand design to commemorate his tomb and so he called Michelangelo to Rome in March 1505 to discuss possible designs. From the beginning, the relationship between Michelangelo and Julius was a tempestuous one, peppered by many arguments between two equally volatile and determined men. A deep-rooted respect for each other eventually grew between the two men and this survived in Michelangelo long after the death of Julius II.

The tomb project proved to be a millstone about Michelangelo's neck. He had hoped that it would be a grand and astonishing masterpiece, a magnificent reminder—not just of a great and powerful pope but also of his own genius. Michelangelo was never to be allowed to dedicate himself to the tomb; he was repeatedly taken off the project to work on others. The first such occasion was by Julius' own insistence that he should work on the Sistine Chapel, temporarily abandoning the tomb. The later uprisings in Florence also contributed to Michelangelo's inability to fulfil the contract.

DESIGN FOR THE TOMB OF POPE JULIUS II (1505–45)
Celimage.sa/Scala Archives

*T*HE original design for the tomb of Julius was for a free-standing block about 50 ft high, with three stories containing niches that were to house more than 40 statues. There was to be an internal room for the remains of the pope. The top storey was to have gigantic statues, twice life-size, of figures such as *Moses* (1513–16).

Condivi, one of Michelangelo's biographers, called the project "the tragedy of the tomb" and Michelangelo himself felt that he wasted his youth over it, intermittently spending 40 years on the project. Following the pope's death in 1513, the contract for the tomb was taken up by his family and there were allegations that Michelangelo had cheated Julius out of a substantial amount of money. This upset Michelangelo deeply, particularly as the fate of the tomb had largely been taken out of his hands; often one of his patrons would wrangle with another over which project he was to take on next.

After several revisions, arguments, and court cases, the tomb was completed with only three statues by Michelangelo: *Moses, Rachel,* and *Leah,* the last two produced between 1542 and 1559.

MOSES (DETAIL FROM THE TOMB OF POPE JULIUS II) (1513–16)

Celimage.sa/Lessing Archive

EASILY the most impressive piece on the tomb of Pope Julius II is the majestic *Moses*. Reminiscent of *The Prophet Ezekiel* (1508–12) with his fierce expression and gigantic proportions, *Moses* stands out against the other more diminutive and tame statues on the tomb. Completed between 1513 and 1516, this huge statue is more than twice life-size. In the earlier designs for the tomb, *Moses* was initially intended to take a place on the second tier of what was to be a three-tier, 50-ft structure among five other statues of the same size. This intention explains the incongruous size and the fierce expression of *Moses*: he was meant to be seen at a distance, from below, which would have made these factors less apparent.

Moses was the greatest figure of the Old Testament, deliverer of the Children of Israel out of Egypt to the Promised Land. Under his right arm he holds the tablets of law given to him by God. On his head are two horns; this convention dates from medieval times as a result of a mistranslation of Hebrew text. He should have rays of light emanating from his head.

RACHEL AND LEAH (DETAIL FROM THE TOMB OF POPE JULIUS II) (1542–55)

Celimage.sa/Scala Archives

*I*N the Old Testament, Rachel was the younger and more attractive daughter of Laban. Jacob loved her and worked for seven years under Laban in order to marry her. He was deceived into marrying her sister, Leah, and served Laban for a further seven years before being finally allowed to marry Rachel, only to find that she was barren. After persuading Jacob to sleep with both Leah and her servant Bilhah, Rachel prayed to God, who heard her pleas and "opened her womb." She died in childbirth.

Aside from the Biblical description of this story, Michelangelo derived much from the interpretation that Dante Alighieri (1265–1321) gave the two sisters in *Purgatorio*; that of Active and Contemplative life. To illustrate the idea of contemplation, Michelangelo shows a serene Rachel gazing up toward heaven with her hands clasped in prayer. He also used the notion of Active life in his sculpture of *Giuliano de' Medici*. With *Leah*, the Active element is portrayed by the mirror she holds, symbolizing the sentiment with which we must contemplate our actions. While *Giuliano de' Medici* embodies the idea of the Active life through his expression and posture, Leah's posture seems more to embody the Contemplative life, as she is slightly slumped and seems deep in thought.

DYING SLAVE (1513–16)
Celimage.sa/Lessing Archive

*T*HE *Dying Slave* was one of twelve sculptures of slaves that Michelangelo originally intended to be housed in the *Tomb of Pope Julius II.* This statue, together with the *Rebellious Slave* (1513–16), are the only two that appear near completion; both sculptures are now in the Louvre in Paris.

The *Slaves*, in much the same way as the *Ignudi* in the Sistine Chapel, were designed to be decorative figures along the base of the tomb as it was originally designed. They were to be placed against columns and pilasters or on the corners of the tomb, but after many revisions and rescalings, the figures were found to be too big for their planned niches. The figures of *Rachel* and *Leah* (1542–55) were carved and the rest, such as the *Young Slave* (1520–30), were abandoned in what may be their incomplete state, although many critics believe that Michelangelo intended them to be left freely carved.

The sculpture of the *Dying Slave* has a sensual, erotic quality. Michelangelo has created the semblance of a reclining figure in a vertical position. The left arm is held above the tilted head and the other arm lies limply upon the breast—the figure appears to be in a dreamlike state rather than actually dying.

REBELLIOUS SLAVE
(1513–16)
Celimage.sa/Scala Archives

*P*OPE Julius II summoned Michelangelo to Rome to commission him to design his tomb. What should have been the most prestigious commission of his career, a freestanding tomb with some 40 figures, to be located in St Peter's, became, in Michelangelo's own words, the "tragedy of the tomb." Julius died in 1513, the contract was redrawn several times over the following years with ever-diminishing funding, other demands were made on Michelangelo by successive popes, and the project was finally cobbled together in 1545, a shadow of its original conception, with much help from assistants, in S. Pietro in Vincoli (Julius's titular church). The tomb is now principally famous for the colossal figure of Moses (c. 1515), one of Michelangelo's greatest sculptures.

Two slave figures, *Dying Slave* and *Rebellious Slave* (c.1513), intended for the tomb, are now in the Louvre, in Paris. These unfinished slaves reveal Michelangelo's sculptural process, in which the figure would be outlined on the front of the marble block and then worked steadily inward from one side of the block. Those parts that projected farthest were brought to a fairly finished state, with those parts farther back remaining rough-hewn. In this way the figures of the slaves appear to be struggling to be free.

Rebellious Slave, originally intended for the tomb of Pope Julius II, is an evocative and poignant testimony to the sculptor's ability to convey emotion through the medium of stone.

YOUNG SLAVE (1520–30)
Celimage.sa/Scala Archives

LIKE the *Dying Slave* (1513–16), the *Young Slave* seems to be slumbering. His head is hidden in the crook of his arm, with his hand loosely clenched, appearing to be softly described within the rough marble. Michelangelo's method of working from the front of the block of marble first is demonstrated here by the protrusion of the *Young Slave's* bent leg. The angle of the leg means that the calf is behind the knee, and therefore still within the block of marble, waiting for Michelangelo's chisel to bring it into being.

By the positioning of his raised arm, the *Young Slave* appears to be struggling, as if held behind his back by unseen forces. His torso twists with the movement of his arm so that it is slightly off-center.

Although the *Slaves* share the similarly contorted poses of the *Ignudi* (1508–12), this particular statue lacks the elegance of the latter; the limbs of the figure are thick and heavy. Whether this is to do with the incomplete state of the figure or with Michelangelo's attempt to represent a slave trapped in marble is a question for endless debate.

VICTORY (1519–30)

Celimage.sa / Scala Archives

*T*HE *Victory* statue may have been intended as another *Slave* for the *Tomb of Julius II* (1505–45), but was carved later than the others, after another revision of the contract for the tomb with Pope Leo X. Victory is one Michelangelo's most influential sculptures; the spiral form and the unnatural, self-conscious pose were much simulated among the Mannerist artists that he helped to inspire.

The sculpture has a triangular configuration like that of the *Doni Tondo (Holy Family)* (1504). The spiral movement can be seen starting with the defeated, crouched figure, rising through the knee of the victor and carrying on through his twisted torso to his turned head. This mimics the form and movement of a serpent and gained the name *figura serpentinata*.

A spiraling form in sculpture encourages the creation of a free-standing piece that can be viewed from every angle. However, with *Victory*, this was not to be the case. It was planned to stand against the tomb of Julius II. Michelangelo may have intended his sculpture to be viewed from the front only, but now it can be viewed freely all round and stands up well to that scrutiny.

HEAD (DETAIL FROM VICTORY) (1519–1530)
Celimage.sa/Scala Archives

AS with much of Michelangelo's work, many opinions have been offered as to the meaning behind the *Victory* statue. The victorious, but curiously mild-looking, youth has been put forward as the soul who has conquered the old man, thus representing mortality. Other opinions suggest that the old man is Michelangelo himself and that the young man symbolizes the suffocating demands of his patrons. The head of the old man does indeed bear some resemblance to the Michelangelo we see in portraits and he did suffer endless problems with demanding patrons changing their minds about his commissions or fighting among themselves and with him.

Another suggestion from critics is that the statue may symbolize youth conquering the progress of age. Michelangelo was approaching middle age when this piece was carved; the youth's arrogant and overly self-confident appearance, with his vacuous stare and conceited pose, have been used to back up this theory.

THREE VIRILE NUDES (DATE UNKNOWN)
Celimage.sa/Scala Archives

*D*URING the High Renaissance, the three outstanding artists were Leonardo da Vinci, Raphael (1483–1520), and, of course, Michelangelo. All three Italian artists worked within similar areas, shared the same patrons and, often, the same locations. In his *Study for the Doni Madonna* (1503), Michelangelo successfully recreated the manner and techniques of Leonardo da Vinci and this study is a reproduction of work by Raphael.

While Michelangelo worked on the Sistine Chapel ceiling, Raphael was painting frescoes for one of the papal rooms in the Vatican, the Stanza della Segnatura (1508). Michelangelo viewed Raphael as an enemy; he was the nephew of his professional rival, Bramante, and, with his sociable, extravagant lifestyle, was the antithesis of Michelangelo's meager, isolated life; during this period the latter claimed "I have no friends, nor do I want any."

After Michelangelo had completed the narrative panels in the Sistine Chapel, Bramante sought permission for his nephew Raphael to complete the work; a request that both distressed and angered Michelangelo. In a letter dated 1542, more than 20 years after the death of Raphael, Michelangelo claimed that all the arguments between himself and Julius II were caused by Bramante and Raphael, blaming them for his inability to complete the pope's tomb, and saying of Raphael "all he had of art he owed to me."

INTERIOR OF THE MEDICI CHAPEL (1519–34)

Celimage.sa/Scala Archives

*I*N 1520, Michelangelo began work, at the request of Pope Leo X, on the interior of the New Sacristy of the San Lorenzo Chapel in Florence. San Lorenzo was the private chapel of the Medici family and the New Sacristy was built to house the bodies of four of the Medici clan, of which Leo X himself was a member. Michelangelo kept the design for the New Sacristy in line with Filippo Brunelleschi's (1377–1446) design of the Old Sacristy in the same church, built about 100 years earlier.

The chapel has eight doors, two on each wall, of which five are façades that were added to make the remarkable symmetry of the interior possible. Above each door is a niche created purely for decoration. The windows in the second storey of the chapel have been given heavy pediments and are narrower at the top than at the bottom; this gives them an increased perspective to make the walls appear higher than they are.

The pilasters, cornices and pediments are all a dark-gray *pietra serena*, a fine-grained sandstone, to accentuate the white marble of the walls. The contrast between the two is enhanced by the light that enters through the many windows of the three-tiered building.

NIGHT (1520–34)
Celimage.sa/Lessing Archive

*T*HE figure of *Night* sits on the sarcophagus of Giuliano de' Medici. She lies with her eyes closed, as if asleep, her head bowed, resting against her hand. She wears a crown decorated with a moon and stars. Crouched in the crook of her leg is an owl, a further allusion to the state of night. Nighttime and sleep have long been poetically linked to—and used as euphemisms for—death, so the sculpture of *Night* is particularly apt for a funeral chapel.

This figure, although graceful and exquisitely poised, again shows Michelangelo's misunderstanding of the female form through the unrealistic, misshapen breasts of the statue, which are too far apart. As with the *Cumaean Sibyl* (1508–12), the flaw in his depiction of the female form can be blamed on the fact that he did not use female models in his work and probably never slept with a woman.

In response to admiration of the statue, Michelangelo wrote the following poem:

> *"Dear to me is sleep, and better to be stone,*
> *So long as shame and sorrow is our portion.*
> *Not to see, not to feel is my great fortune;*
> *Hence, do not wake me; hush, leave me alone."*

DAY (1520–34)
Celimage.sa/Lessing Archive

THE partner to the statue of the slumbering *Night* is the ponderous figure of *Day*. With his huge head raised to look over one muscular shoulder, Day echoes the impression of alertness that *Giuliano* above him gives. His posture is the opposite of his partner *Night*: where her legs are closed to the viewer and her chest is open, *Day's* legs are open and the chest is closed. These postures reflect the different attributes of the sculptures; in sleep we are exposed and vulnerable while awake we can control our vulnerabilities.

Day is sitting in a complicated, crossed, and twisted position; his left arm can be seen behind his back, the hand pointed toward the viewer. This huge figure seems impossibly balanced upon the sarcophagus, as if he is in danger of sliding off. As with all of the statues on top of the tombs, *Day's* feet hang precariously over the edge. The base of the statue remains rough and unfinished, in contrast to the smooth limbs and torso. A further more noticeable contrast lies in the unfinished head of the piece, only barely formed, seeming to suggest in stone the vagaries of light and the ambiguity of time, reminiscent of the face of the *Bearded Slave* (1520–30).

LORENZO OF URBINO (1520–34)
Celimage.sa/Scala Archives

*L*ORENZO *of Urbino,* like *Giuliano of Nemours,* sits in his niche with his gaze directed toward the *Madonna and Child* (1520–34). As Giuliano is alert and appearing ready to move toward the Madonna, Lorenzo's pose is somber and introverted. He has one hand to his mouth and his head is bowed, as if he is deep in thought as he gazes at the Madonna. *The Madonna and Child* was originally planned to adorn the tombs of Lorenzo the Magnificent, the grandfather of the two dukes, and his brother Giuliano, so the fact that they are both gazing in that direction may have as much to do with deference toward their ancestors as religious piety.

Michelangelo again used Classical idealized features on the statue, rather than attempting a likeness of the duke. The slightly larger figure of Lorenzo sits less easily than Giuliano within the confines of his niche; his posture means that he takes up more space. *Lorenzo of Urbino* also shares the Roman body armor of his counterpart. His helmet is positioned low on his head so that his eyes are almost lost within the shadows of the niche he occupies.

DAWN (1520–34)

Celimage.sa/Scala Archives

*T*O reflect the representation of *Lorenzo of Urbino* as contemplative, Michelangelo placed the figures of *Dawn* and *Dusk* underneath the statue. The personification of these indeterminate, hazy times of day acts to symbolize the hesitant, inactive nature of Lorenzo as Contemplative life. To emphasize the aspects of *Dawn* and *Dusk*, the original lighting in the chapel was dimmed by the use of shaded windows on the side of Lorenzo's tomb. These shadings have since been removed so that light in the chapel is now consistent.

   Dawn exudes a most sorrowful air. Seemingly full of woe, she also appears confused, as if she has just awoken and is bitterly disappointed to be in a conscious state again. The band round *Dawn's* chest and the veil on her head were both signs of mourning which, together with her expression of dismay, gives us the impression that she is in the throes of grief. Perhaps *Dawn* is grieving over the death of Lorenzo, whose sarcophagus she reclines upon, or maybe she grieves over the existence and inevitability of death itself. *Dawn* opens her eyes from her disturbed dreams to see the symbol of death, *Night*, as she lies asleep on the tomb opposite her.

DUSK (1520–34)
Celimage.sa/Scala Archives

DUSK, like the statue of *Day*, may be incomplete. The body has been highly finished and the smooth marble is polished, but his face is still pitted with the marks of Michelangelo's chisel. This lack of finish does nothing to detract from the magnificence of Michelangelo's creation.

Dusk lies with his legs stretched out in front of him and his arms relaxed down by his sides in an open posture, leaving his body softened and exposed. His partner *Dawn* shares this position and both figures act to contrast the contorted poses of *Night* and *Day* that appear opposite them. Both *Dawn* and *Dusk* seem even more precariously balanced upon the sarcophagus than the figures of *Night* and *Day* do, as their relaxed legs extend farther over the edge.

The age of *Dusk* reflects the time of day he represents, while the figure of *Dawn* is young. *Dusk's* head is bowed, *Dawn's* uplifted—alluding to the rising and setting of the sun. The four statues represent the inexorable passing of time and the inevitability of death.

LAURENTIAN LIBRARY, READING ROOM (C. 1524–34)

Celimage.sa/Scala Archives

THE Medici family were not only great collectors of art, between them they had also compiled an extensive library of precious books and rare manuscripts. In 1519, the Medicean Pope Clement VII decided that a suitably grand library should be built to house this collection, which had been started by Cosimo de' Medici during the fifteenth century.

The design of the Laurentian Library above the refectory in the San Lorenzo monastery followed that of the library in San Marco convent, also in Florence. Situating a library on the upper floor of the building meant that the natural lighting was improved and any potential damage from damp was limited.

As the library was to be built on top of the existing refectory as an extra storey, it was necessary to make the structure as light as possible in order to minimize the strain on the building below. The walls of the reading room are very thin, painted in a white stucco. Michelangelo used the same *pietra serena* sandstone for the supporting structures, pilasters, cornices, and window frames of the reading room that he used in the Medici Chapel (1519–34). The tilted, ornate wooden desks were also designed by Michelangelo.

APOLLO (C. 1530)

Celimage.sa/Lessing Archive

MICHELANGELO began this statue of Apollo, sometimes called *David*, between 1528 and 1530, for Baccio Valori, who was a political nominee of the Medici family. In 1530 they fought to regain power over the city of Florence from the republican government that had formed after they were expelled in 1527. Michelangelo had allied with the Florentine republicans and helped their cause by building fortifications for the besieged city and consequently was not popular with the Medici. *Apollo* may have been a diplomatic commission to appease any feelings of resentment that Valori held against Michelangelo. The piece was left in an unfinished state when he returned to Rome after the death of his father in 1534; it was never completed.

The sculpture employs a twisting form, a lesser *figura serpentinata* than *Victory* (1519–34), but still evidently serpentine—from the bent leg through to the tilt of the torso and the turn of the head. The artist had explored bodies in twisted movement with the *Ignudi* (1508–12) in the Sistine Chapel and in much of his sculpture.

DETAIL FROM APOLLO (C. 1530)
Celimage.sa/Lessing Archive

GIORGIO Vasari, a biographer of Michelangelo, claimed that the unfinished *Apollo* has one arm raised to reach and pull out an arrow from a quiver that was to be positioned on his back. Seen from this angle, there is a noticeable block of marble still remaining unformed but unremoved across and down Apollo's shoulder, which could possibly have been intended to be a quiver of arrows.

When *Apollo* is seen in entirety, the lack of finish of the sculpture does not detract from the graceful, liquid stance and the perfect naturalism used for the body of the god. Observed in detail, however, the lack of finish becomes more obtrusive. The head of *Apollo* is pitted with Michelangelo's chisel marks. His features are lacking in expression and character, his eyes sealed blindly shut.

The face of the bearded man in the statue of *Victory* (1519–30) has been completed to a much higher degree than *Apollo*. In comparison, it becomes clear that the facial expressions of Michelangelo's marble statues were created at a late stage in their metamorphosis.

HERCULES AND CACUS (1525–28)

Celimage.sa/Scala Archives

IN Classical mythology, Cacus, the son of Vulcan, stole Hercules' cattle, hiding their destination by dragging them by their tails. Upon finding his herd, Hercules fought and strangled Cacus. This is a classic tale of good triumphing over evil, and the piece was commissioned by the Signoria (republican governors) of Florence following the ousting of the Medici family in 1527. Likewise *David* had been commissioned after the republican uprisings of 1494, and it was intended that the two pieces should be placed together as a permanent reference to the might of the republic over the fallen Medici.

The block of marble intended for the piece had been quarried in Carrara before 1508 and was assigned to Michelangelo. He never used this marble, since it was later given to Baccio Bandinelli (1493–1560), an arch-rival of Michelangelo, who made the flawed *Hercules and Cacus* that now stands in front of the Palazzo Vecchio in Florence.

Michelangelo usually used small, three-dimensional models in wax and clay as part of his sketching process. This figure of *Hercules and Cacus* shows that Michelangelo intended to create a statue to be viewed from every angle. The arm of Cacus wraps round the legs of Hercules, whose legs point in the same direction, encouraging the viewer to walk round the piece.

IDEAL HEAD (C. 1533)
Celimage.sa/Scala Archives

*T*HE *Ideal Head* is one of many drawings made by Michelangelo for his friend and probable lover, Tommaso de' Cavalieri, a beautiful young nobleman. He was one of the few people Michelangelo drew, claiming that most people's features were too imperfect, but Cavalieri's beauty made him exceptional. The drawings were intended to help Cavalieri as an artist, so that he could study the master's hand. *Ideal Head* is a black-and-red chalk drawing of Michelangelo's concept of the ideal of beauty. The features are drawn from his imagination, as with the similar drawing of *Zenobia* (c. 1533).

During Michelangelo's lifetime, love (platonic or otherwise) between men was not deemed as subversive as it was by the end of the century; even so, there were caustic comments about his affections for the young nobleman. His poems to Cavalieri were altered by later publishers to decrease the amorous affection within them, in lines such as:

> *"Your will includes and is the lord of mine;*
> *Life to my thoughts within your heart is given;*
> *My words begin to breathe upon your breath:*
> *Like to the moon am I, that cannot shine*
> *Alone."*

STUDY OF A MAN SHOUTING (C. 1533)
Celimage.sa/Scala Archives

*T*HE *Study of a Man Shouting* is a good example to art students on how to create vivid and intense expressions. The sketch shows in great detail the movement of every muscle that takes place when shouting. The veins on the man's neck stand out angrily, as does his Adam's apple. The muscles on his forehead are clenched together in a frown. Michelangelo evoked the form of the face using charcoal as a medium.

By drawing material and hair swirling as if they are being blown around the man's face, Michelangelo has given the impression that he is attempting to shout into a violent wind. This is a simple device that was used on the Sistine Chapel ceiling to create the illusion of movement or, as with the *Delphic Sibyl* (1508–12), to give the idea of a forbidding wind blowing through the scene.

The fierce facial expression that many of Michelangelo's older men wear, also seen in the *The Creation of the Planets, the Sun, and the Moon* (1508–12), has been characterized as the *terribilità*, and is generally interpreted as a reflection of Michelangelo's own tormented, turbulent emotions.

THE DEAD CHRIST (BASED UPON A STUDY FOR THE PIETÀ FOR THE GOVERNOR OF MILAN) (1533–54)
Celimage.sa/Lessing Archive

KNOWLEDGE of human anatomy was greatly limited in the sixteenth century and information that any art student can take for granted today was not available. Studies of medicine and anatomy increased throughout the Renaissance but were still uncommon. Much of what isolated Michelangelo as a genius and artist beyond compare, was the supreme naturalism that he displayed in his depiction of nudes. As can be seen in this sketch, and in the *Studies for a Flying Angel* (1536–41), every muscle was intently studied and perfected before he began to paint or sculpt his chosen image.

Michelangelo's outstanding representation of the human form was not derived simply from an astute observation of his models. In his late teenage years, following the death of Lorenzo the Magnificent, Michelangelo studied human anatomy. A prior at a local hospital allowed him access to the corpses, and Michelangelo spent many grim hours dissecting these bodies to gain an understanding of the muscles, ligaments, and frame that make human movement possible. It was study that, according to his biographer Ascanio Condivi, left Michelangelo with a damaged appetite: "He gave up dissecting corpses because long handling of them had so affected his stomach that he could neither eat nor drink salutarily."

THE LAST JUDGMENT (1536–41)
Celimage.sa/Scala Archives

*P*OPE Julius II had originally conceived the idea of covering the altar wall of the Sistine Chapel in St Peter's, Rome, with a depiction of the Resurrection of Christ, a theme that would have complemented the ceiling's overall theme of the creation and downfall of Man. The plans for the altar wall reemerged following a fire that damaged the altarpiece by Pietro Perugino. Pope Paul III, who appointed Michelangelo as his chief painter, sculptor, and architect, gave him the commission for the fresco in 1534. At the time, Michelangelo was yet again trying to complete the doomed project of the *Tomb of Pope Julius II* (1505–45), but Paul III intervened, insisting that the artist should work on his projects instead.

The altar wall is 40 ft wide by 45 ft high, making *The Last Judgment* the largest undivided work of art to be undertaken by a single individual. At what point the theme of the Resurrection became *The Last Judgment* is unclear, although it is most probable that Pope Paul III, a strong reformist, influenced the change. The theme was a fitting one for Rome, recovering as it was from several murderous attacks both on the city and on the papacy, that had led to famine, poverty, and plague.

DETAIL OF THE BLESSED
(FROM THE LAST JUDGMENT) (1536–41)
Celimage.sa/Scala Archives

WITHIN the mass of crowded figures in *The Last Judgment* there is much movement; bodies are seen struggling, fighting, and tumbling in various directions, but the whole painting has a definite sweeping circular movement which is clearly visible. The main motion within the piece begins on the bottom left, with the dead rising up from their graves, floating up to join the blessed on their ascent to Heaven, circling the figure of Christ, then swarming down with the sinners as they descend into Hell. This gives the huge fresco a sense of order.

Among the crowd of the blessed, some figures float upwards with no apparent effort, while most have to struggle to make their ascent or are pulled up by the figures standing on the clouds. On the right, a figure pulls two people up using a rosary, an obvious allusion to the salvation of prayer. The varying efforts of the blessed, while ensuring that the left side of the fresco did not appear static in comparison with the violent movement on the right, illustrates the belief that the path to Heaven is a difficult one, although for a few it seems naturally easy.

STUDY FOR THE LAST JUDGMENT
(DATE UNKNOWN)
Celimage.sa/Scala Archives

MICHELANGELO employed the same preparatory habits for *The Last Judgment* fresco that he used while painting the ceiling frescoes. Several studies have survived that demonstrate his habit of sketching a figure in the position envisioned, before copying this outline onto fresh plaster and then painting. He studied the movement of muscles that occurred in the chosen pose, as well as the perspective and shading necessary to portray the body in that position realistically.

The Christ figure dominates the study as it stands powerfully above the melange of bodies. Desperation and reverence combine within the skillfully drawn scene to convey an evocative detail from the Last Judgment. The subsequent adaptation of the final painted work is faithful to the chaotic intertwining of the human forms depicted in this study.

The theme of *The Last Judgment* as Michelangelo has handled it, with the mass of flying, tumbling, twisting bodies, gave the artist an ideal arena to explore the varying movements and postures of a body in motion. Michelangelo once claimed that he never used the same pose twice, and the huge variety of figures in *The Last Judgment* would seem to back up this claim.

DETAIL OF ST BARTHOLOMEW
(FROM THE LAST JUDGMENT) (1536–41)
Celimage.sa/Scala Archives

*T*HE saints appear huge, looming over the twisted masses beneath them. Their appearance is partly due to techniques of perspective: as they were painted higher up the wall, their size was increased so they would not appear too small to the viewer on the floor. Each of the saints holds the instruments of their martyrdom; here St Bartholomew sits astride a cloud holding his own skin—he was flayed to death.

As the saints look up toward Christ they thrust the tools of their martyrdom toward him, demanding recognition for their suffering. Although they are already among the blessed, it appears that the saints are fearful of Christ's judgments. Their expressive angst serves to increase the tensions within the piece.

The flayed, gray skin that St Bartholomew holds contains a self-portrait of Michelangelo. This ironic gesture proves to be prophetic when viewed in the light of the arguments that surrounded *The Last Judgment*. When asked by Pope Paul III to make the fresco "more suitable," following comments that it would be more fittingly displayed in a brothel, Michelangelo replied, "make the world a suitable place and the painting will follow suit."

PIAZZA DEL CAMPIDOGLIO (C. 1538)
Celimage.sa / Scala Archives

*T*HE Piazza del Campidoglio sits upon the Capitoline Hill in Rome. While St Peter's is the heart of the religious center of the city, the Campidoglio is the heart of the civic center. Michelangelo's designs for the Campidoglio reclaimed Rome's glorious past; the Capitoline Hill was the center of the Roman Empire, but by the Renaissance it had fallen into ruins.

Michelangelo began work on the Piazza del Campidoglio in 1537–38. He was initially asked by Pope Paul III to create a new pedestal for the Classical statue of Emperor Marcus Aurelius. The statue was then placed in the center of the piazza and became the central focus of Michelangelo's plans, with an oval of patterned pavement spreading out around it, although the pavement was not completed to Michelangelo's design until the twentieth century.

At the back of the piazza is the Senate building which was the Roman Tabularium; on the right is the fifteenth-century Palazzo Conservatori. To create symmetry within the piazza, Michelangelo designed a third palace on the left and façades for the Senate and the Conservatori. This idea of a symmetrical, balanced town center was novel at the time, yet it was perhaps Michelangelo's most influential architectural design and has been widely copied throughout the world.

BUST OF BRUTUS (C. 1542)

Celimage.sa / Lessing Archive

*W*HILE still working on *The Last Judgment*, Michelangelo began work on a marble bust in the Classical Roman Imperialist style that had previously been reserved for emperors and the wealthy. The bust was commissioned by a friend of Michelangelo who, like himself, had helped defend the city of Florence from the siege by the Medicis. It is thought that the bust may have been made to commemorate the murder of tyrannical Alessandro de' Medici by his cousin Lorenzino in 1537. Alessandro was hated by the Florentine exiles in Rome, who fled the city after the Medicis regained their power, and his murder was likened to that of Caesar by Brutus in 44 BC. An alternative inspiration is noted as an imperial portrait bust of the Roman emperor Caracalla, who reigned from 211 to 217 AD.

The features for the face were taken either from an ancient portrait believed to be of Brutus or from the bust of Caracalla. The piece is unfinished and as a result the thick neck appears strangely large if viewed from the front, set as it is against such finely draped robes. With the Classical Roman features and side profile, the bust bears some resemblance to the statue of *Giuliano de' Medici* (1520–34), but Brutus appears stronger, more determined and lacks the slight arrogance seen in the face of Giuliano.

SACRIFICE OF ISAAC (DATE UNKNOWN)
Celimage.sa / Scala Archives

G OD told Abraham to take his son Isaac to the land of Moriah and offer him as a burnt offering. So Abraham cut the wood for the burnt offering, rose early in the morning, and took two men to accompany him and Isaac close to the place of sacrifice. Then he cut wood for the burnt offering, built an altar, bound Isaac and laid him upon it, and covered him with wood. He was just about to slay his son with the knife, but was stopped by the angel of the Lord. Abraham's dutiful willingness to sacrifice his son secured his reputation as the first Jewish patriarch.

In this evocative sketch the artist captures the dramatic biblical episode and poignantly depicts the fear and blind faith of the subjects. The delicate drawing shows the fearful Abraham being startled by the intervention of the angel of the Lord. Michelangelo gives a sensitive treatment to a highly charged episode through fine line and soft tones.

HEAD OF CHRIST (C. 1540)

Celimage.sa/Scala Archives

*T*HIS *Head of Christ* is a partial fragment of a sculpture that Michelangelo worked on during the 1540s. The sculpture was of a *Pietà* scene with a similar structure to that of the later *Rondanini Pietà* (c. 1556–64), which shows the body of Christ being supported by the Madonna standing behind him. This was a vision of the *Pietà* that Michelangelo was never able to successfully portray in marble, although sketches survive that show us his intentions for this unusual rendering of the scene.

There are many unfinished sculptures by Michelangelo. As was evident in the *Tomb of Pope Julius II* (1505–45), his patrons would often disrupt his work on particular projects and his own life often interrupted his work too. Many scholars have suggested that Michelangelo would abandon a piece when he found that he had achieved the intimation of the expression he had been searching for; that pieces such as the *Abandoned Slaves* (1520–30) embody within their unfinished form the heart of the artist's vision. Unlike his contemporaries, Michelangelo rarely made use of assistants. Despite this, he accepted many large commissions that overlapped, leaving their completion a physical impossibility for himself.

227

STUDY OF MADONNA AND CHILD
(WITH ST JOSEPH) (DATE UNKNOWN)
Celimage.sa / Scala Archives

*T*HE last works of Michelangelo were invariably religious in content, reflecting his deepening sense of spirituality. From his work as an architect at St Peter's in Rome, through to his final Pietà sculptures and drawings, Michelangelo seems to have been seeking redemption through his art. It was as though he were trying to find some visual expression of intense religious and personal beliefs. This drawing revisits the theme of the Madonna and Child, treated in his famous sculpture at Bruges, and other works such as his *Pitti Tondo* and the *Taddei Tondo*.

Michelangelo's treatment of the Madonna and Child with St Joseph offers an unusually intimate group portrait. All three figures are loosely connected in a touching intimacy, which nevertheless pays attention to the formalities of anatomical drawing. The Virgin Mary offers protection to an unusually plausible infant, who seems to play nonchalantly as he rests upon her knee.

MARY MAGDALENE CONTEMPLATING THE CROWN OF THORNS (DATE UNKNOWN)
Celimage.sa/Lessing Archive

*T*HIS lovely drawing is astonishing for its sheer beauty. It represents Mary Magdalene, who had supported Mary the Mother of Christ after the deposition following the crucifixion. Mary Magdalene is obscured by the legends that surrounded her following the Resurrection and there is considerable difference of opinion as to her identity. She was the woman exorcized of seven devils, she ministered to the Lord in Galilee, and was among the women present at the crucifixion of Christ. With Joanna and Mary, the mother of James, and Salome, she discovered the empty tomb and heard the angelic announcement of the Resurrection of Christ. She was said to be the first person to see Christ later that same day.

Mary Magdalene Contemplating the Crown of Thorns is an intense and moving portrayal of despair as the young woman grieves, clutching the fallen crown. The natural pose lends an authenticity to this work.

THE CONVERSION OF ST PAUL (1542–45)
Celimage.sa/Lessing Archive

UPON completion of *The Last Judgment* (1536–41) in the Vatican, Pope Paul III asked Michelangelo to decorate his private chapel, the Capella Paolina, which was adjacent to the Sistine Chapel and in which popes were selected at that time. Michelangelo began in 1542 with *The Conversion of St Paul*, a theme chosen in deference to Paul III. Before his vision of God and subsequent conversion to Christianity, Paul was a Pharisee named Saul who was traveling along the road to Damascus to murder the Christians who lived there. Although historically St Paul was young, here he is depicted as an old man of a similar age to the pope.

The *Conversion* fresco was begun shortly after the unveiling of *The Last Judgment*, but the coloring within the piece shares more with that used in the ceiling of the Sistine Chapel. In the *Conversion*, the colors are bright and varied, with none of the drabness that invades *The Last Judgment*. The whole fresco is infused with the light that the figure of Christ directs at St Paul.

Despite the many figures within the work, the viewer's attention is focused on two figures: that of St Paul as he lies on the ground, and on Christ as he hurls himself down from the Heavens, with a blazing light in his path. Michelangelo reverted to a more traditional portrayal of Christ here than in *The Last Judgment*.

THE CRUCIFIXION OF ST PETER
(1542–50)
Celimage.sa / Lessing Archive

*T*HE *Crucifixion of St Peter* was chosen as decoration for Pope Paul III's private chapel in the Vatican because in Christian tradition Peter was the first pope and therefore father of the new Church.

There is a circular motion within *The Crucifixion of St Peter* akin to that in *The Last Judgment* (1536–41). The figures are all placed in a wide circle round the central figure of Peter. People point to Peter to emphasize the focus on him and the women in the near foreground direct the gaze to him with turned heads and wide-eyed stares. Michelangelo increased the intensity of the light within the center of the picture to further focus the viewer's attention on the figure of St Peter.

Four men are preparing to stand the cross that bears the saint. St Peter chose to be crucified upside down, and in order to avoid compositional difficulties, Michelangelo chose to show the cross as it is about to be erected so that St Peter is able to pull himself up to glare fiercely out at the viewer. The impact of his accusatory stare outward enhances the fact that he is the focus of everybody else in the painting.

INNER COURTYARD, PALAZZO FARNESE (BEGUN 1547)

Celimage.sa / Scala Archives

*T*HE Farnese Palace in Rome was mainly built to the designs of Antonio da Sangallo the Younger, who also worked on St Peter's. He began work on the Palace in 1517 and by his death in 1534, the building had reached the second storey, with the façade almost complete. The completion of the palace was thrown open to a public design competition in 1547; Michelangelo's successful design included an additional third storey for the inner courtyard of the palace and the large cornice that now surmounts the façade.

In the courtyard, Sangallo's middle storey is clearly much more traditional than the ornate, grandiose style Michelangelo employed for his third storey. The windows are surmounted by heavy, arched pediments, decorated with a ram's head placed centrally in each and garlands flowing from either side. These pediments do not connect with the windows but rest upon the capitals that crown the pilasters. On top of the window frames are lion's heads. The columns that flank the windows of the second storey have become dominating pilasters by the third storey. Michelangelo also altered the second storey by adding triangular pediments and the entablature decorated with a garland motif.

INTERIOR OF THE DOME OF THE BASILICA OF ST PETER'S (BEGUN 1546)
Celimage.sa / Scala Archives

*T*HE original Basilica of St Peter dates from 324 AD. It was built in honor of St Peter on top of his burial site. In the early fifteenth century the original cathedral was torn down and replaced by the church we see today. The construction was a slow, lengthy process. Julius II sought out the artist Bramante, who didn't complete his work on the structure. Raphael, Antonio da Sangallo, Petuzzi, and Michelangelo were selected to continue constructing the basilica. They incorporated their ideas with some of those of Bramante and Rosselli.

In 1547 Pope Paul III entrusted the design of the dome on St Peter's Basilica to the 72-year-old Michelangelo, who had turned down the job half a century earlier. Though he didn't finish the project, he played a large role in making St Peter's the magnificent home of art and beauty that it is today. Domenico Fontana and Guglielmo Della Porta finished the job between 1585 and 1590.

The architectural makeup of St Peter's Basilica is one of grandiose proportions. Five entrance portals lead into the church. Michelangelo projected a dome in a slightly pointed form. As with Brunelleschi's Florence dome, the pointed shape exerts less thrust. It is believed that the dome's astounding size is greater than Michelangelo had planned. It sweeps to an awesome height and allows a cycle of light to stream through the windows inset below the Cupola.

DUOMO PIETÀ (C. 1547–55)

Celimage.sa/Lessing Archive

MICHELANGELO worked on the *Duomo Pietà* intermittently for seven years. He carved it for his family tomb as a fitting memorial for himself and the family he loved so well. By 1547 he was 70 years old and the knowledge of his own mortality was evidently important in this work. The sculpture is housed in the Museo dell' Opera del Duomo in Florence and is sometimes called *The Deposition of Christ*, as is the painting of *The Entombment*, which illustrates a similar scene.

The man at the back supporting the body of Christ is Nicodemus, who was a follower of Jesus and, together with Joseph, helped take down his body from the cross. He was also a sculptor who carved the visions that God sent him; poignantly Michelangelo has given Nicodemus his own features.

The deformed left arm of Christ has clearly been broken in several places and his left leg is missing altogether. According to Vasari, Michelangelo was deeply discouraged both by the *Pietà* and his own failing abilities, and attacked the statue in a fit of frustration. He later gave the *Pietà* to his assistant Tiberio Calcagni, who attempted to finish it; the incongruous figure on the right, Mary Magdalen, is attributed to his weak craftmanship.

STUDY FOR THE HOLY FAMILY (EPIFANIA) (C. 1553)
www.heritage-images.com / The British Museum

*T*HERE is much mystery surrounding the cartoon of the *Holy Family (Epifania)*; it is unclear why this large preparatory drawing was produced and equally uncertain what the cartoon is depicting. It was later used by Ascanio Condivi, Michelangelo's friend and biographer, as the basis for his version of the painting.

The central figure is the Virgin Mary, who shelters Christ beneath her legs. The other child is St John the Baptist. On her left, Mary pushes away Joseph, whose features are clearly a self-portrait by Michelangelo. Mary is in deep discussion with the androgynous figure on her right, who leans toward her. There are several other outlines of faces within the cartoon, which are also leaning toward Mary, as if straining to hear the discussion.

One explanation of the cartoon's subject is that the surrounding vague outlines are the half-brothers and half-sisters of Christ, who were Joseph's children from an early marriage. The androgynous figure may be St Julian, who was renowned for his chastity and may be encouraging Mary's continuing chastity, hence her pushing Joseph away.

STUDY FOR CHRIST ON THE CROSS (WITH THE VIRGIN AND ST JOHN) (1562–64)

Celimage.sa/Lessing Archive

*T*HIS crucifixion scene is one of several that Michelangelo worked on during his final years. It uses the medium of pencil and black chalk on paper. At one point Michelangelo intended to make a fitting memorial to his great friend Vittoria Colonna, who died in 1547, and it is possible that some of the crucifixion drawings are designs made for this purpose.

On the right is the hazy figure of St John, his mouth agape, eyes wide as if in dismay, much like the expressions of some of the sinners in *The Last Judgment* (1536–41). All three figures have been sketched and reworked as Michelangelo strived for the ideal postures that he was seeking. As a result of this reworking, their outlines are blurred and both the Virgin, who stands on Christ's right, and St John appear to have double images behind them, giving the picture a haunting quality.

The design of the cross means that Jesus' arms are high above his head. This placement is echoed by the form of Mary, who stands with her arms crossed protectively against her chest. Michelangelo altered the picture to make this possible and the original position of her arm is easily seen.

PALESTRINA PIETÀ (C. 1556)

Celimage.sa / Scala Archives

THE *Palestrina Pietà* is so named because it was originally placed in Palestrina, having been cut from a marble that was found only close to this small town. Michelangelo is believed to have made the statue around 1556, although its authenticity has been questioned. The *Pietà* was first documented in Palestrina in the seventeenth century. At the least, it is probable that other sculptors added their own touches to the piece, or that Michelangelo started the sculpture, which was then carried on in his style by an apprentice.

The composition of the *Palestrina Pietà* bears a great resemblance to that of the earlier *Duomo Pietà* (*c.* 1547–55). Both pieces are unusual in that the *Pietà* traditionally depicts the Madonna and Christ alone. In both statues, the body of Christ leans heavily against the figures that try to support him; his head is tilted and his legs fold underneath him.

The *Palestrina Pietà* is in a lesser state of completion than the *Duomo Pietà*. Only the body of Christ has been partially completed; as was common with Michelangelo, the torso and upper limbs are almost finished, while the lower limbs are still barely freed from the marble.

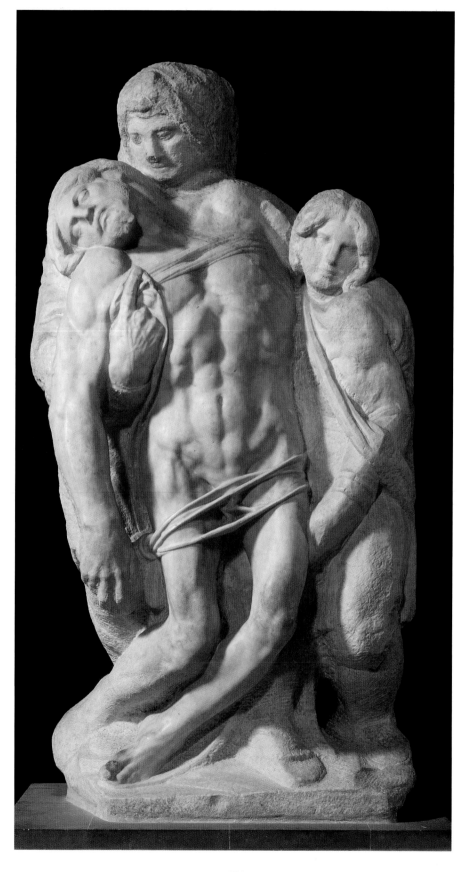

HEAD OF CLEOPATRA (C. 1553)

Celimage.sa/Scala Archives

DURING the Ptolemaic Period there were several queens in Egypt named Cleopatra; the most famous and influential in history was the seventh. Cleopatra's beauty was surpassed only by her charm and ambition. Despite her political acumen, she had notably contributed to the fall of both Julius Caesar and Marc Antony. After her defeat by Octavius, the land of Egypt came under Roman domination.

Cleopatra was that last sovereign of the Macedonian dynasty, and although she had no Egyptian blood, she proclaimed herself Daughter of Ra, the Sun God of Egypt. She dedicated her efforts to enforcing her royal status as queen of Egypt, restoring the glories of Ptolemy and recovering Egypt's dominions in southern Syria and Palestine, as well as sharing in the central Roman authority.

Head of Cleopatra is a powerful aristocratic portrait. It evinces the seductive and vulnerable beauty of the legendary queen whose death by suicide is a theme touched on by artists and writers alike. This classical study of the female head allows us to see the natural evolution from portrait sketch to sculpted stone used to great effect by the artist. The pose and the vacant eyes give a sculptural quality rather than a formal portrait effect to the image.

THE RONDANINI PIETÀ (C. 1556–64)

Celimage.sa / Scala Archives

*T*HE *Rondanini Pietà* (named after the palace where it was housed) was the final sculpture on which Michelangelo worked. He was working on the sculpture up to six days before his death. Working with marble takes considerable strength; although Michelangelo was almost 90 by this time, he was in the habit of carving a little of the *Pietà* each day.

The *Rondanini Pietà* differs from other of Michelangelo's *Pietàs* in that the figure of the Madonna is standing on a raised level, the body of Christ leans back against he,r and she supports his body from behind. Michelangelo's frustration with the erosion of his sight and skills is keenly felt within the piece. The bodies and scale of the two figures bear no relation to the lower legs of Christ or to the dismembered right arm that can be seen on the left. It is possible Michelangelo became unhappy with the sculpture and began decreasing the scale, starting from the top, to create smaller figures from the block.

ST PETER'S BASILICA (BEGUN 1546)

Celimage.sa/Scala Archives

EMPEROR Constantine (c. 288–337 AD) built the original St Peter's church over his tomb in the fourth century. Pope Julius II initially commissioned Michelangelo's great rival Bramante to renovate the building, but as the structure had deteriorated, the architect began to demolish the old building and created designs for a new, grand church. Bramante died in 1514 and was replaced by several successive architects, including his nephew Raphael. Pope Paul III approached Michelangelo in 1546 following the death of Sangallo the Younger; although reluctant, Michelangelo accepted the commission in 1547.

Bramante died leaving incomplete plans for St Peter's, which were modified by later architects. Despite his intense dislike of Bramante, Michelangelo chose to return to much of his original design, rejecting Sangallo's later plans. The workers on St Paul's held allegiance to Sangallo, having worked under him for many years, and Michelangelo's changes made him unpopular. He justified himself by saying that Bramante's designs were "not full of confusion, but clear, pure, and full of light, so that it did not in any way damage the palace...whoever departs from this order of Bramante's, as Sangallo has done, departs from the truth."

ST PETER'S BASILICA (1546–1564)

Celimage.sa / Scala Archives

ICHELANGELO once remarked lightheartedly that "one could expect to see the last day of the world sooner than see St Peter's finished." He would accept no payment for his work on the basilica, and viewed the project as spiritually redeeming. During the 17 years he spent working on St Peter's, the building work was considerably progressed and by the time of his death in 1564, a large part of the drum that the cupola rests on had already been erected.

Following Michelangelo's death, Pope Paul III set a brief that his designs for St Peter's were still to be adhered to, but as few clear or instructive plans were left by the artist to show his intentions, later architects made various changes to the building. One major change in design was the form of the nave being changed from the Greek cross plan of Michelangelo's and Bramante's to the Latin cross design that can now be seen.

Overall, however, Michelangelo did succeed in setting the style of the building. The cupola was completed after his death, largely to his design. The columns and rectangular windows with their arched pediments are reminiscent of his work in the Piazza del Campidoglio.